CHEMISTRY MAGIC

Learning Chemistry Through Fun-Filled Experiments

Edward Palder

Illustrated by Gary Mohrmann

ISBN: 0-933149-18-2 (cloth)
ISBN: 0-933149-25-5 (pbk)

Cover Design and Illustration: Gary A. Mohrmann
Book Design and Typesetting: Wordscape, Inc., Washington, D.C.

Manufactured in the United States of America

2 3 4 5 6 7 8 9 10

For information about institutional purchases and other Woodbine House
books, please send for a free catalog:
  Woodbine House
  10400 Connecticut Avenue
  Kensington, Maryland 20895
Call Woodbine House's Toll-Free Number **(800) 843-7323**

To every reader whose
imagination combines magic
with science.

Table of Contents

Chapter 3
Magic with Ultraviolet Light..61

Chapter 4
Chemical Magic with Time 73

Chapter 5
Cold Light Chemical Magic....79

Chapter 6
Creative Crafts Magic 87

Chapter 7
Chemical Magic Grab Bag 121

Glossary 151

Foreword

Chemistry Magic includes my newest collection of exciting chemistry and chemistry-related experiments that are safe, easy to do, and easy to understand. I have chosen experiments that you can use to dazzle audiences as well as learn from. There is a world of fascination ahead for you as you learn the basics of chemistry while becoming a skilled magician.

Some of the experiments appear in print in this book for the first time, while others have been adapted from the secrets of years long past (from those master magicians of yesteryear who amazed and mystified audiences with their magical powers). And finally, there are a few experiments from unknown sources, their origins lost with the passing of time.

Easy, step-by-step directions walk you through the experiments. We begin with "Effect" that describes the purpose of the experiment, then "Materials" that you will need, followed by directions in the "What To Do" section. The experiment concludes, in most cases, with "What Happens," a simple explanation of how the experiment works. In some experiments there are "Suggestions" for doing the experiment in other ways. Using this format, *Chemistry Magic* illustrates scientific principles to introduce you to the wonderful world of chemistry and demonstrate some of the things you can do with your new knowledge.

You can do all the experiments at home in a basement laboratory, in the kitchen, or in the backyard. You can learn about chemistry while having the fun and excitement of performing an experiment for a science club demonstration, doing a science fair project, a school research project, or just experimenting on your own. Many of your experiments can be adapted into magic routines for entertaining audiences while others can be used to create interesting arts and crafts objects and other useful items.

The experiments are not complicated and do not require special equipment. Best of all most of them require only easy-to-obtain materials that cost only a "few pennies." To be part of the fun that *Chemistry Magic* offers, all you need is curiosity, imagination, and the desire to learn. You will discover that chemistry is both an important science and an adventure.

Edward L. Palder

Chemistry Do's and Don'ts

There are two rules to working with chemicals.

1. BE CAREFUL

2. USE YOUR COMMON SENSE

Although the experiments in this book are safe and easy to perform, when you work with chemicals you should always take certain precautions.

Before Beginning:

Read The Instructions. Don't change or skip any steps. Be sure to wear goggles or gloves if the experiment calls for them.

Plan Ahead. Have all materials ready before starting.

Always Work Under Adult Supervision.

If You Don't Understand the Experiment, check with your parents or teacher.

After Beginning:

Be Careful Not To Splash Any Solution In Your Face Or Eyes.

Never Taste, Drink, or Smell any chemicals or mixtures.

Never Change the amount of chemicals called for, unless specifically instructed.

Don't Substitute one chemical for another.

Be Patient. Don't rush to finish an experiment.

Always Follow any special instructions.

Don't Touch chemicals with your hands unless the instructions say to do so.

Always Clean Up when you're finished. Unless special instructions are given, flush liquids down the sink with running water. Discard solids in a trash can with a tight cover.

Never Save Solutions. Always Make Fresh.

Store chemicals and equipment in a locked cabinet or box.

Where To Get Chemicals and Equipment

Many of the experiments in *Chemistry Magic* can be performed with materials and equipment used in your home, school, or purchased locally. Some hobby supply stores have science departments that feature chemicals in small quantities. The following list will identify where supplies can be obtained. For items not available locally, write to the companies listed under MISCELLANEOUS CHEMICALS AND EQUIPMENT, or check your telephone directory for science supply outlets in your area.

From the Drug Store

Acetone...alum...ammonium chloride...ammonium hydroxide...aspirin tablets...beeswax...benzoin tincture...calcium chloride...castor oil...chalk (calcium carbonate)...copper sulfate (blue vitriol)...95% denatured alcohol...dextrose...distilled water...ferric chloride tincture...fluorescein...fluorescein sodium...formalin solution...glucose liquid...glycerin...gum arabic...hydrochloric acid...hydrogen peroxide...iodine crystals...iodine tincture...kaolin...lanolin...litmus paper...magnesium sulfate (Epsom salts)...mercurochrome solution...methylene blue...petroleum jelly (Vaseline)...phenolphthalein...phenolphthalein sodium...plaster of Paris...potassium bromide...potassium permanganate...potassium thiocyanate (potassium sulfocyanate)...quinine sulfate...silver nitrate...sodium benzoate...sodium bicarbonate...sodium carbonate...sodium iodide...sodium salicylate...sodium silicate solution (egg preserver)...sodium thiosulfate...tannic acid...white paraffin (wax)...wintergreen oil (methyl salicylate).

From the Grocery Store

Dilute acetic acid (white vinegar)...aluminum foil...dilute ammonium hydroxide (soapless household ammonia)...borax (e.g., Boraxo; 20-Mule Team Borax)...charcoal briquets...cooking oil...corn oil...cream of tartar...distilled water...food colors...gelatin...laundry dye (e.g., Rit; Tintex)...laundry starch liquid...laundry starch lumps...nonrising flour...nonfat milk powder...olive oil...rice flour...salt (sodium chloride)...skim milk...soap flakes (e.g., Ivory Snow)...soap liquid...sodium bicarbonate (baking soda)...sodium bisulfate (e.g., Sani Flush)...sodium chloride (salt)...sodium hypochlorite (laundry bleach)...sugar...yeast...yellow laundry soap...white paraffin (wax).

From the Hardware Store

Calcimine paint...cement...charcoal briquets...dry glue...hydrochloric acid (muriatic acid)...lacquer...linseed oil...liquid glue...liquid white glue (e.g., Elmer's Glue)...marble dust...plaster of Paris...rosin...sand...shellac...spackle mixture...spar varnish...wallpaper paste...whiting.

From An Artist Supply or Craft/Hobby Shop

Dry earth colors...lacquer...linseed oil...litharge...plaster of Paris...prepared India yellow...prepared madder lake...shellac...spar varnish...tempera paints...ultramarine blue...white lead.

For Miscellaneous Chemicals and Equipment

- CHEMICAL SHED, P.O. Box 748, San Bernardino, CA 92402-0748 (Catalog $2)
- CHEM-LAB SUPPLIES, 13814 Inglewood, Hawthorne, CA 90250 (Catalog $1)
- HAGENOW LABORATORIES, 1302 Washington, Manitowoc, WI 54220 (Catalog $1)
- MERRELL SCIENTIFIC, 1665 Buffalo Road, Rochester, NY 14624 (Catalog $2)
- PIONEER INDUSTRIES, 14A Hughey Street, Nashua, NH 03060 (Catalog $1)
- VARA SCIENTIFIC, P.O. Box 1677, Newark, NJ 07102 (Free catalog)
- YOUNG-EDISONS, 934 South 13th, Manitowoc, WI 54220 (Catalog $1)

For Cold Light Chemical Magic

DISTILLATION PRODUCTS INDUSTRIES, Eastman Kodak Company, Rochester, NY 14603
FISHER SCIENTIFIC COMPANY, 711 Forbes Avenue, Pittsburgh, PA 15219 (Check the telephone directory for depots in other cities)

For Ultraviolet Light Experiments

U.V.P. INC., 5100 Walnut Grove Avenue, San Gabriel, CA 91778
Also available from arts and crafts stores, artist supply stores and hobby shops.

How To Prepare Solutions

Percentage Solutions

Some experiments require solutions with a specific strength. In many cases, a balance is needed to prepare them. If you don't have a balance, ask your local pharmacist to weigh out the chemicals (he might be willing to prepare the solutions). Dissolve the chemical in three-fourths of the liquid called for. Then add sufficient liquid to make the solution up to the required volume. Always use the percent figure to equal the number of grams that will be dissolved in 100 cc of finished solution. For example, dissolve 10 grams (10% x 100 cc) in 75 cc (¾ of the volume being prepared), and continue as explained above. To make a 1% solution, use 1 gram; 5%, use 5 grams; 30% use 30 grams, etc. For less than 100 cc, divide everything by 2 to make 50 cc; by 4 to make 25 cc, etc. To make more than 100 cc, multiply instead of divide.

Dissolving Two or More Chemicals

To prepare a solution using more than one ingredient, divide the liquid in equal amounts, one for each chemical and proceed as above. Combine the solutions and follow any instructions as to the order of mixing.

Adding Other Chemicals

When the instructions call for you to make the solutions acid or basic, or to add a preservative, the amounts to be added are usually small and can be disregarded with reference to the final volume.

Using Heat to Dissolve Chemicals

Never use heat to help dissolve chemicals unless the instructions specifically say to do so.

How To Prepare Saturated Solutions

A saturated solution contains as much solid as will dissolve in a given amount of liquid at a specific temperature, usually room temperature. Add an excess of the solid to the liquid with stirring. Let stand for 24 to 48 hours. Keep covered. If any solid remains undissolved, the solution can be considered saturated. If none remains, add more and let stand for 24 hours. Avoid temperature changes. At lower temperatures, less solid will dissolve; at higher temperatures, more will be required. Filter and store the solution in a tightly sealed bottle.

Preparation of Dilute Acid Solutions

Always add the acid to the water very slowly, never the water to the acid.

Preparation of Phenolphthalein Solution

Dissolve 0.5 gram of phenolphthalein in 25 cc of 95% denatured alcohol and add 25 cc of distilled water.

Special Instructions

The subject matter of this book is scientific in part. I have been as specific in directions, explanations, and warnings as possible. You must follow these directions directly as I have given them to you. If you don't, your experiments may not work out properly. I have attempted to limit the experiments to those that require chemicals that are safe to handle. Where special methods are necessary for safe handling of chemicals, I have included explicit instructions and warnings.

Be sure to read the information under CHEMICAL DO'S AND DON'TS before starting any of the experiments. Also, the reference to water, wine, ink, milk, etc., in some of the experiments, is for the purpose of magic presentations only. THEY ARE NOT THE REAL THING AND SHOULD NOT BE TASTED, SMELLED, OR CONSUMED.

CHAPTER 1

Color Changing Solutions

Imagine a pitcher filled with water that you are able to change, upon command, to wine, milk, ink, or other colored liquids. Then, as if by magic, you change them to something else. These changes appear to be a demonstration of secret powers. But you know that they are only simple chemical reactions combined with showmanship and a touch of mystery.

Historical evidence about ancient civilizations reveals that magic and chemistry played significant roles in introducing people to the excitement of the unknown. Even today chemistry continues to dazzle us with inventions of miraculous wonders, some appearing almost magical in effect. By following the instructions for this chapter's experiments, you can amaze your audience with marvelously entertaining and mystifying illusions.

NEVER TASTE, DRINK, OR SMELL ANY OF THE CHEMICALS OR MIXTURES

A Magic Pitcher

✳ The Effect:

Empty glasses are filled with water that changes to wine, ink, and milk.

✔ You Will Need:

Ferric chloride tincture; 10% sodium carbonate solution; 5% tannic acid solution; benzoin tincture; phenolphthalein solution.

◇ Preparation:

Fill an opaque glass pitcher with 8 ounces of phenolphthalein solution and 25 ounces of tannic acid solution.

Arrange 6 glasses:

No. 1	Leave unprepared
No. 2	1 tsp sodium carbonate
No. 3	Leave unprepared
No. 4	10 drops ferric chloride
No. 5	½ tsp benzoin
No. 6	1 tsp sodium carbonate

✱ Presentation:

Fill the glasses with the solution from the pitcher. Water will appear in glasses 1 and 3, wine in glasses 2 and 6, ink in glass 4 and milk in glass 5.

▭ What Happens:

Glasses 2 and 6 contain a base (sodium carbonate) that reacts with phenolphthalein. Phenolphthalein, an indicator, turns red with a base. The blue color in glass 4 is a complex iron compound. The milk in glass 5 is a benzoin precipitate, and in glasses 1 and 3, left unprepared, water appears.

Water To Wine To Water

✸ The Effect:

This is an old favorite among magicians in which water changes to wine, and the wine to water.

✔ You Will Need:

Dilute acetic acid; phenolphthalein solution; sodium carbonate.

◇ Preparation:

Arrange 3 glasses:

No.1	8 drops phenolphthalein, 4 oz. water
No. 2	⅛ tsp sodium carbonate, 1 tsp water
No. 3	2 tbsp acetic acid

✸ Presentation:

Empty glass 1 into glass 2 to produce wine. Pour the wine into glass 3 and it will change to water.

⊃ What Happens:

Phenolphthalein, an indicator, turns red with a base (sodium carbonate) and colorless in acid (acetic acid). Excess acid neutralizes the base, making the solution acid.

Double Change I

✳ The Effect:

Fill an empty glass with a wine colored liquid that changes to water and back to wine.

✔ You Will Need:

Sodium carbonate; phenolphthalein solution; sodium bisulfate.

◇ Preparation:

Arrange 2 glasses:

No. 1	6 drops phenolphthalein, ⅛ tsp sodium carbonate, 6 oz water
No. 2	¼ tsp sodium bisulfate, 1 tbsp water

✷ Presentation:

Slowly pour the wine from glass 1 into glass 2. It will change to water. Stop a few seconds to show the water. Continue to fill glass 2 and the water changes back to wine.

⤸ What Happens:

Phenolphthalein, an indicator, turns red with a base (sodium carbonate) and colorless in acid (sodium bisulfate). Sodium bisulfate neutralizes the base, making the solution acid. Excess carbonate neutralizes the acid, making the solution basic.

Double Change II

✳ The Effect:

Fill an empty glass with water that changes to wine and back to water.

✔ You Will Need:

Sodium carbonate; phenolphthalein solution; sodium bisulfate.

◇ Preparation:

Arrange 2 glasses:

No. 1   6 drops phenolphthalein,
             ¼ tsp sodium bisulfate,
             6 oz water
No. 2   ⅛ tsp sodium carbonate,
             1 tbsp water

✳ Presentation:

Slowly pour the water from glass 1 into glass 2. It will change to wine. Stop a few seconds to show wine. Continue to fill glass 2 and the wine changes back to water.

⤇ What Happens:

Phenolphthalein, an indicator, is colorless in acid (sodium bisulfate) and turns red in a base (sodium carbonate). Sodium carbonate neutralizes the acid, making the solution basic. Excess sodium bisulfate neutralizes the base, making the solution acid.

Classic Wine and Water Trick

✳ The Effect:

From my personal repertoire of chemical magic taken from the master magicians of long ago, I give you this next effect—another mystifying illusion in which water changes to wine, back to water, again to wine and once more to water.

✔ You Will Need:

10% sodium hydroxide solution; 10% sodium bisulfate solution; phenolphthalein solution.

◇ Preparation: Wear Goggles

Fill a glass pitcher with 9 glasses of water and ¾ teaspoon phenolphthalein.

Arrange 9 glasses:

1	Leave unprepared
2	6 drops sodium hydroxide
3	Leave unprepared
4	6 drops sodium hydroxide
5	Leave unprepared
6	6 drops sodium hydroxide
7	30 drops sodium bisulfate
8	2 tsp sodium hydroxide
9	2 tbsp sodium bisulfate

✳ Presentation:

Fill glasses 1 through 7 with the solution from the pitcher. In glasses 1, 3, 5, and 7 water will appear, and wine in glasses 2, 4, and 6. Empty them into the pitcher. Fill glasses 1 through 8 to produce water in the first seven glasses and wine in glass 8. Again, empty into the pitcher. Fill all nine glasses to produce wine in the first eight glasses and water in glass 9. Once more empty into the pitcher and fill all of the glasses. This time water appears in the glasses.

⬛ What Happens:

Phenolphthalein, an indicator, turns red with a base (sodium hydroxide) and colorless in acid (sodium bisulfate). Sodium bisulfate neutralizes the sodium hydroxide in glasses 2, 4, and 6 making the solution acid. The sodium hydroxide in glass 8 neutralizes the sodium bisulfate and the solution turns basic. In glass 9, the sodium bisulfate neutralizes the sodium hydroxide, making the solution acid.

◆

Wine, Water, and Ink

✳ The Effect:

Five glasses filled with water changes to wine, ink, and back to water.

✔ You Will Need:

Ferric chloride tincture; dilute ammonium hydroxide; 10% sodium sulfocyanide solution; 10% tannic acid solution; 15% oxalic acid solution. Make only 5 or 10 ml.

◇ Preparation: Wear Goggles and Gloves

Fill a glass pitcher with five glasses of ammonium hydroxide.

Arrange 5 glasses:

1	10 drops ferric chloride
2	4 drops sodium sulfocyanide
3	10 drops sodium sulfocyanide
4	15 drops tannic acid
5	1 oz oxalic acid

✳ Presentation:

Fill glass 1 with the liquid from the pitcher to produce water. Pour the water into the pitcher and fill glass 2 to produce wine. Again empty the glass into the pitcher and fill glass 3. Red wine will appear. Repeat and fill glass 4 to produce wine. Repeat once more, filling glass 5 and water will appear. Empty into the pitcher and fill all five glasses to produce water.

▭ What Happens:

Chemical reactions produce color changes. (Note: It might be necessary to adjust the sodium sulfocyanide in glasses 2 and 3 to produce satisfactory colors.)

National Colors

✺ The Effect:

Three glasses are filled with water that changes to red, white, and blue.

✔ You Will Need:

Phenolphthalein solution; 5% lead nitrate solution; 5% copper sulfate; dilute ammonium hydroxide.

◇ Preparation: Wear Goggles

Arrange 3 glasses:

1	15 drops phenolphthalein
2	15 drops lead nitrate
3	15 drops copper sulfate

✳ Presentation:

Starting with No. 1, fill the glasses with the solution in the pitcher. The colors red, white, and blue appear.

⬮ What Happens:

In glass 1, phenolphthalein, an indicator, turns red with a base (ammonium hydroxide). In glasses 2 and 3, chemicals react to produce color changes.

* ＊

✔

◇

＊

▭

Water to Wine

＊ The Effect:

Two glasses filled with water mysteriously produce one with water and the other with wine.

✔ You Will Need:

Ferric ammonium sulfate; 10% sodium salicylate solution.

◇ Preparation:

Fill a glass pitcher with 16 ounces of water in which 1 teaspoon of ferric ammonium sulfate has been dissolved.
Arrange 2 glasses:

1	Leave unprepared
2	¼ tsp sodium salicylate, 2 tsp water

＊ Presentation:

Fill the glasses with the solution from the pitcher. Water will appear in glass 1 and wine in glass 2.

▭ What Happens:

In glass 1, left unprepared, a reaction does not take place and water appears. The red color in glass 2 is a complex iron compound.

The Mysterious Pitcher

✳ The Effect:

Five glasses are filled with water that changes to wine and back to water.

✔ You Will Need:

Sodium carbonate; dilute acetic acid; phenolphthalein solution.

◇ Preparation: Wear Goggles

Fill an opaque glass pitcher with 5 glasses of water.
Arrange 5 glasses:

1	⅛ tsp sodium carbonate
	2 tsp water
2	Leave unprepared
3	8 drops phenolphthalein
4	Leave unprepared
5	4 tsp acetic acid

✳ Presentation:

Fill glasses 1 through 4 with water from the pitcher. Empty into the pitcher and refill to produce wine in glasses 1 through 4, and water in No. 5. Empty into the pitcher. Refill again and water appears in all the glasses.

▭ What Happens:

Phenolphthalein, an indicator, turns red with a base (sodium carbonate) and colorless in acid (acetic acid). Acetic acid neutralizes the sodium carbonate making the solution acid.

✳

✔

◇

✳

▭

Water To Ink To Water I

✳ The Effect:

Water changes to ink and back to water.

✔ You Will Need:

Ferric ammonium sulfate; tannic acid; oxalic acid.

◇ Preparation: Wear Goggles

Arrange 3 glasses:

1	⅛ tsp ferric ammonium sulfate, 6 oz water
2	pinch of tannic acid 15 drops water
3	1 tsp oxalic acid, 3 tsp water

✳ Presentation:

Empty glass 1 into glass 2 to change the water to ink. Pour the ink into glass 3 and it changes to water.

▭ What Happens:

Chemical reactions produce color changes.

Water To Ink To Water II

✳ The Effect:

This is one of my favorites. It is certain to mystify your audience as they see you change water to ink and ink back to water.

✔ You Will Need:

Sodium carbonate; sodium ferrocyanide; ferric ammonium sulfate.

◇ Preparation: Wear Gloves

Fill an opaque glass pitcher with 5 glasses of water.
Arrange 5 glasses:

1	⅛ tsp sodium ferrocyanide
2	Leave unprepared
3	⅛ tsp ferric ammonium sulfate
4	Leave unprepared
5	6 tsp sodium carbonate 2 oz water

✳ Presentation:

Fill the glasses with water from the pitcher. Five glasses of water will appear. Empty glasses 1 through 4 into the pitcher. Refill to produce ink. Empty the five glasses into the pitcher. Refill, and water appears once more.

▭ What Happens:

Chemical reactions produce color changes.

◆

21

※

✔

◇

※

▭

Supernatural Pitcher

※ The Effect:

This is another favorite of mine in which six glasses are filled with water that changes to different colors.

✔ You Will Need:

Ferric ammonium sulfate; potassium thiocyanate; barium chloride; potassium ferrocyanide; tannic acid; tartaric acid; sodium bisulfite.

◇ Preparation: Wear Gloves

Fill a glass pitcher with 18 ounces of water in which slightly more than 1 teaspoon of ferric ammonium sulfate has been dissolved.

Arrange 6 glasses, each with 2 teaspoons of water, and add ⅛ teaspoon of:

1	potassium thiocyanate
2	barium chloride
3	potassium ferrocyanide
4	tannic acid
5	tartaric acid
6	sodium bisulfite

※ Presentation:

Fill the glasses with the solution from the pitcher. In glass 1, a red color appears; in glass 2, a white color; in glass 3, a blue color; in glass 4, a black color; in glass 5, a green color; and in glass 6, an amber color.

▭ What Happens:

Chemical reactions produce color changes.

Water To Wine– To Beer–To Milk

✳ The Effect:

This is one of those effects in which the unexpected occurs. Water changes to wine, the wine to water, then to beer, and to milk.

✔ You Will Need:

Dilute acetic acid; phenolphthalein solution; 5% silver nitrate solution; liquid soap; iodine tincture; sodium chloride; sodium carbonate.

◇ Preparation: Wear Goggles and Gloves

Fill an opaque glass pitcher with 8 glasses of water in which 1 teaspoon of sodium chloride and 2 teaspoons of sodium carbonate have been dissolved.

Arrange 8 glasses:

1	1 tbsp acetic acid
2	5 drops phenolphthalein
3	1 tbsp acetic acid
4	5 drops phenolphthalein
5	1 tbsp acetic acid
6	5 drops phenolphthalein
7	2 tbsp soap, 4 drops iodine
8	1 tsp silver nitrate

✳ Presentation:

Fill glasses 1 through 6 with the solution from the pitcher. Water will appear in glasses 1, 3, and 5; and wine in glasses 2, 4, and 6. Empty into the pitcher. Fill all the glasses, this time producing water in glasses 1 through 6, beer in glass 7, and milk in glass 8.

⤳ What Happens:

In glasses 1, 3, and 5 phenolphthalein, an indicator, is colorless in acid (acetic acid). In glasses 2, 4, and 6 it turns red with a base (sodium carbonate). The acetic acid neutralizes the sodium carbonate, making the solution acid. This causes water to appear when the glasses are filled a second time. The beer in glass 7 is a mixture of iodine and

✳

✔

◇

✳

⤳

Notes

the foam is from the soap. In glass 8, the milk is silver chloride, a result of the silver nitrate reacting with sodium chloride. (Stir when filling glasses 7 and 8, to produce the foam in 7, and to prevent the precipitate in 8 from settling to the bottom.)

Vanishing Blue Color

✳ The Effect:

In this next effect you explain that there are some liquids with nervous properties, and when irritated they undergo unexpected changes. Show a bottle of water, shake it and suddenly the water turns blue. Letting it rest, the blue color disappears and the water reappears. The effect can be repeated.

✔ You Will Need:

Potassium hydroxide; methylene blue; dextrose; distilled water.

◇ Preparation: Wear Goggles

Dissolve 5 grams of potassium hydroxide in 250 ml water. Add 3 grams of dextrose and a pinch of methylene blue. USE A SPATULA TO HANDLE POTASSIUM HYDROXIDE AND METHYLENE BLUE. Pour into a glass bottle with a narrow neck and wide bottom. Close tightly with a rubber stopper.

✸ Presentation:

Pick up the bottle and give it a quick jerk upward. The water will turn blue, remaining for 15 to 20 seconds. Violent shaking will make the blue color last longer. Letting it remain undisturbed, the color will disappear. The effect can be repeated. The solution will keep for only two or three days. Discard and use a fresh solution.

⟳ What Happens:

Air reacts with methylene blue, turning it a blue color. Left to rest, the air escapes and the color disappears.

Spectator's Choice

✳ The Effect:

You can change water to wine, and wine to water.

✔ You Will Need:

Tannic acid; oxalic acid; ferric chloride tincture.

◇ Preparation:

Fill an opaque glass pitcher with 6 glasses of water in which 2 teaspoons of tannic acid have been dissolved.
Arrange 6 glasses:

1	Leave unprepared
2	Leave unprepared
3	4 drops ferric chloride
4	4 drops ferric chloride
5	4 drops ferric chloride
6	2 tsp oxalic acid, 6 tsp water

✳ Presentation:

Ask someone to select either wine or water. If wine is called for, fill glass 3, 4, or 5. If water, fill glass 6. Then, fill the other glasses to produce 3 with wine and 3 with water. Empty the glasses into the pitcher and refill. This time 6 glasses of water will appear.

▭ What Happens:

Chemical reactions produce color changes. In glasses 1 and 2, left unprepared, reactions do not take place.

Magic Bottle

❋ The Effect:

You can pour red wine, water, milk and champagne from the same bottle.

✔ You Will Need:

Ferric sulfate; sodium bisulfate; calcium chloride; sodium bicarbonate; potassium permanganate.

◇ Preparation:

Fill an amber quart bottle with water in which 1 teaspoon of sodium bisulfate and 2 teaspoons of ferric sulfate have been dissolved.

Arrange 4 glasses:

1	Leave unprepared
2	½ tsp calcium chloride
3	pinch potassium permanganate
4	¼ tsp sodium bicarbonate

❋ Presentation:

Fill the glasses with the solution from the bottle to produce water in glass 1, milk in glass 2, red wine in glass 3 and champagne in glass 4.

⤶ What Happens:

In glass 1, left unprepared, water appears. In glass 2 the milk is a suspension of calcium sulfate (calcium chloride reacting with ferric sulfate) that should be stirred to prevent it from settling to the bottom. The wine in glass 3 is a dilute solution of potassium permanganate. In glass 4 the champagne is a solution of carbon dioxide (sodium carbonate reacting with sodium bisulfate).

Magic Colors–Red, Yellow, and Black

✳ The Effect:

In this bewildering effect water turns red, yellow, and black.

✔ You Will Need:

Tannic acid; sodium bisulfite; sodium salicylate; ferric ammonium sulfate.

◇ Preparation: Wear Goggles

Fill a glass pitcher with 3 glasses of water in which 1 tablespoon of ferric ammonium sulfate has been dissolved.
Arrange 3 glasses, each with 2 teaspoons of water, and:

1	⅛ tsp sodium salicylate
2	1 tsp sodium bisulfite
3	¼ tsp tannic acid

✳ Presentation:

Fill the glasses with the solution from the pitcher. The colors red, yellow, and black will appear.

⬭ What Happens:

Chemical reactions produce color changes.

Confusing Colors

✳ The Effect:

This is another effect in which the unexpected happens. Red paper, placed in a red liquid, turns blue.

✔ You Will Need:

Red litmus paper; sodium carbonate; phenolphthalein solution.

◇ Preparation:

Dissolve 1 teaspoon of sodium carbonate in 6 ounces of water. Add a few drops of phenolphthalein to color the solution red.

✳ Presentation:

Place a piece of red litmus paper in the solution. Instead of staying red, the paper turns blue.

⬓ What Happens:

Phenolphthalein, an indicator, turns red with a base (sodium carbonate). Red litmus, also an indicator, turns blue with a base.

Green To Red To Purple

✳ The Effect:

A green liquid turns red and then purple.

✔ You Will Need:

Potassium hydroxide; manganese dioxide; potassium nitrate; distilled water; dry ice.

◇ Preparation: Wear Goggles

Mix and heat to a glowing red (use a porcelain crucible) for three minutes:

> ½ tsp potassium hydroxide
> ½ tsp manganese dioxide
> ½ tsp potassium nitrate

USE A SPATULA TO HANDLE POTASSIUM HYDROXIDE. Let cool. Add 3 tablespoons water to extract the green potassium manganate. Filter and discard the residue.

✳ Presentation:

Dilute the potassium manganate with 3 ounces of water. Drop in a small piece of dry ice. USE PAPER TO HANDLE THE DRY ICE. As the ice dissolves, the solution will appear to boil and it will turn red, then reddish-blue, and finally purple.

⮑ What Happens:

Potassium hydroxide, manganese dioxide, and potassium nitrate react to form green potassium manganate. Carbon dioxide (dry ice) reacts with potassium manganate to form purple potassium permanganate. The color changes occur as the potassium manganate decreases and the potassium permanganate increases.

The Bubbling Caldron

✳ The Effect:

This is a classic master deception of chemical magic in which a boiling liquid mysteriously changes color.

✔ You Will Need:

Universal indicator; dilute ammonium hydroxide; dry ice; distilled water.

◇ Preparation:

Fill a large glass bowl (e.g., fishbowl, brandy snifter, etc.) with slightly warm distilled water. Add 5 to 10 drops of universal indicator and just enough ammonium hydroxide to turn the liquid purple.

✳ Presentation:

Drop in a piece of dry ice. USE PAPER TO HANDLE THE DRY ICE. As the ice dissolves, the water will appear to boil and the purple color will turn blue, then green, and finally yellow.

⬭ What Happens:

Dry ice (carbon dioxide) reacts with water to form carbonic acid that neutralizes the base (ammonium hydroxide). As the acid forms, the acidity of the solution increases and the indicator changes color. In a base universal indicator is purple; in acid it is yellow.

◆

NEVER TASTE, DRINK, OR SMELL ANY OF THE CHEMICALS OR MIXTURES

*

✔

◇

✳

◻

Apple Cider

✳ The Effect:

You explain to your audience that Mother Nature gets very angry if apples are picked before they are ripe. This next effect, you tell them, is her way of punishing people who make cider from unripe apples. When this cider is poured into a glass, it turns green.

✔ You Will Need:

Sodium dichromate; sodium thiosulfate.

◇ Preparation: Wear Goggles and Gloves

Dissolve sufficient sodium dichromate in water to prepare an apple cider colored solution. Prepare a glass with 1 teaspoon of sodium thiosulfate and 1 teaspoon of water.

✳ Presentation:

Fill the glass with the apple cider. It will change to a green color, the same color as unripe apples.

◻ What Happens:

Sodium thiosulfate reacts with sodium dichromate, changing it to the green chromic form.

The Vanishing Red Lemon

✳ The Effect:

This magic marvel can be done without sleight of hand or complicated magical apparatus. It is excellent in a routine of close-up magic. The performer makes a red lemon vanish.

✔ You Will Need:

Three fresh lemons; phenolphthalein solution; dilute ammonium hydroxide; hypodermic syringe and needle.

◇ Preparation:

Mix 1 teaspoon of ammonium hydroxide with ¼ glass of water. Add a few drops of phenolphthalein to make the solution turn red.

✳ Presentation:

Fill a syringe with the red liquid and inject it into a lemon. You ask your audience to remember which one is the red lemon, moving them around. Then ask someone to point out the red lemon. You cut open the lemon selected and show that it is the wrong one. Then cut open the other two and reveal that the red lemon has vanished.

⌐ What Happens:

Phenolphthalein, an indicator, turns red with a base (ammonium hydroxide) and colorless in acid. Lemons contain citric acid that neutralizes the ammonium hydroxide, turning the phenolphthalein colorless.

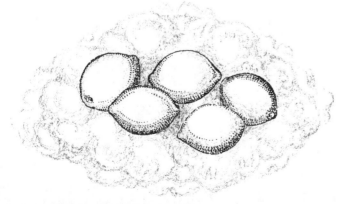

✳

✔

◇

✳

⌐

Water To Wine To Water II

✳ The Effect:

Water turns to wine, and the wine to water.

✔ You Will Need:

Iodine tincture; sodium thiosulfate.

◇ Preparation:

Arrange 2 glasses:

1	10 drops iodine
	15 drops water
2	1 tsp sodium thiosulfate
	2 tsp water

✸ Presentation:

Fill glass 1 with water to produce wine. It might be necessary to adjust the iodine to produce the correct color. Pour the wine into glass 2 and it will change to water.

▭ What Happens:

Sodium thiosulfate reacts with iodine to form a colorless, complex iodine-thiosulfate compound.

CAUTION

Disappearing Purple Color

❈ The Effect:

In this next effect, the "magic" is different in that it takes place slowly as a purple liquid visibly changes to water.

✔ You Will Need:

Sodium bisulfite; sodium bisulfate; potassium permanganate.

◇ Preparation: Wear Goggles

Mix 1 teaspoon of a strong solution of sodium bisulfate with ½ teaspoon of sodium bisulfate. A gas, sulfur dioxide, will form. (This part of the experiment is best done out of doors.) Carefully, without breathing the gas, pour it into a tall glass cylinder.

❋ Presentation:

Slowly pour a solution of potassium permanganate (a few crystals dissolved in 6 ounces of water) into the cylinder. As the potassium permanganate drops to the bottom, it changes to water. If the color does not change, try using a more dilute potassium permanganate solution.

⊃ What Happens:

Chemical reactions produce color changes.

35

Chapter 2

Invisible Ink Magic

The experiments in this chapter are an exciting collection of secrets that describe other ways for you to work with color changing materials to perform chemical magic. There are over 80 experiments focusing on the

"magical" properties of chemicals that makes them invisible under certain conditions and how, through the use of special chemical techniques, you can make them visible. Just as in Chapter I, you will find that invisible ink magic can be very rewarding entertainment for your audience. They'll be amazed! These experiments will set your chemical magic apart from the traditional magic most magicians perform, and will give you countless opportunities for more unusual and different magic.

Invisible inks are chemical compounds that, when written with and allowed to dry, usually cannot be seen. It is only after special treatment—usually using other chemical compounds or changes in the physical environment—can they be made visible. Depending upon how these inks are used, the visibility can be permanent or temporary. Although there are many different kinds of invisible inks, for the most part there are four general categories. These include the inks described in the next four experiments and form the basis for most of the experiments in this chapter.

Heat Sensitive Inks

Simple Inks

The juices from certain foods, when properly prepared, are invisible when written with and allowed to dry. Application of mild heat will develop them as dark writing. A few examples of these juices include:

Lemon juice
Grapefruit juice
Vinegar
Milk
Onion juice
Cabbage juice
Cola drinks

Chemical Inks

Heat can also be used to develop chemical mixtures into visibility. The color of the writing depends upon the chemical compound(s) used. For example:

- Ammonium chloride (1 teaspoon in 6 ounces of water) will produce yellow writing.
- Copper sulfate and potassium bromide (1 teaspoon of each in ½ ounce of water) will develop as yellow writing. Use a light yellow tinted paper to write on.
- Ferric ammonium sulfate (1 teaspoon in ½ ounce of water) will produce brown writing.
- Copper carbonate (⅛ teaspoon) and sodium bisulfate (1 teaspoon) dissolved in water (2 ounces), with the addition of ¼ teaspoon of ammonium chloride will produce green writing. Use a light blue-green tinted paper to write on.

Important–Read First!

ALWAYS

- When using heat to make writing visible, use an oven or iron set at its lowest temperature, an electric light bulb or warm radiator. DO NOT USE OPEN FLAMES.
- Use distilled water to prepare all solutions.
- Use a clean pen for each ink used.
- Store all mixtures in dark, air tight glass bottles in a cool place.

Using A Chemical Developer

The next group of inks uses a second chemical known as a developer. It is applied by spraying, sponging with cotton, or using a blotter. Dissolve each chemical in 2 ounces of distilled water. Store in dark, tightly sealed bottles.

INK	DEVELOPER
Blue Writing	
¼ tsp potassium ferrocyanide	¼ tsp ferric ammonium sulfate
1 tsp copper sulfate	dilute ammonium hydroxide
1 tsp copper sulfate	2 tsp sodium carbonate
½ tsp potassium ferrocyanide	¼ tsp ferric chloride
Black Writing	
1 tsp ferrous sulfate	2 tsp tannic acid
½ tsp lead nitrate	¼ tsp sodium sulfide
¼ tsp silver nitrate	½ tsp sodium sulfide
½ tsp copper sulfate	½ tsp sodium sulfide
¼ tsp ferric chloride	½ tsp tannic acid
Red Writing	
1 tsp sodium carbonate	phenolphthalein solution
½ tsp sodium ferrocyanide	½ tsp copper sulfate
½ tsp ferric ammonium sulfate	½ tsp sodium salicylate
½ tsp potassium thiocyanate	¼ tsp ferric chloride
Yellow Writing	
½ tsp lead nitrate	1 tsp sodium iodide
½ tsp lead acetate	½ tsp potassium chromate
Green Writing	
½ tsp cobalt chloride	1 tsp potassium ferrocyanide
½ tsp copper-chloride	½ tsp cobalt chloride
½ tsp sodium chloride	½ tsp copper sulfate

Wear Goggles and Gloves When Preparing These Experiments

Using Water As A Developer

This next group of invisible inks includes mixtures of dry chemicals that are applied to unsized paper with a soft brush or cotton. Unused inks should be stored in tightly sealed glass bottles. The ink (writing) will become visible when water is used as an ink. A clean pen should be used for each ink.

Blue Writing

1 tsp ferric ammonium sulfate and 1 tsp potassium ferrocyanide
1 tsp potassium ferrocyanide and 1 tsp ferrous sulfate
½ tsp ferric chloride and 1 tsp potassium ferrocyanide

Black Writing

1 tsp ferrous sulfate and 2 tsp tannic acid
¼ tsp ferric chloride and ½ tsp tannic acid
1 tsp tannic acid and ½ tsp ferric ammonium sulfate

Red Writing

1 tsp sodium ferrocyanide and 1 tsp copper sulfate
1 tsp ferric ammonium sulfate and 1 tsp sodium salicylate
½ tsp potassium thiocyanate and ¼ tsp ferric chloride
1 tsp ferric ammonium sulfate and ¼ tsp potassium thiocyanate

Yellow Writing

½ tsp lead nitrate and 1 tsp sodium iodide
1 tsp potassium chromate and 1 tsp lead acetate

Brown Writing

½ tsp ferrous sulfate and 2 tsp sodium carbonate
½ tsp potassium ferrocyanide and 1 tsp copper sulfate
1 tsp ferric ammonium sulfate and 1 tsp sodium carbonate

Green Writing

½ tsp cobalt nitrate and 1 tsp potassium ferrocyanide
1 tsp copper chloride and 1 tsp cobalt chloride
1 tsp sodium chloride and 1 tsp copper sulfate

> **Wear Goggles and Gloves When Preparing These Experiments**

40

The Magic Drawing

✻ The Effect:

This is a classic among chemical magic illusions. Writing disappears, only to be replaced by a picture.

✔ You Will Need:

Potassium iodide; cornstarch; washable blue ink; sodium hypochlorite bleach; 5% hydrochloric acid.

◇ Preparation: Wear Goggles

Dissolve ⅛ teaspoon of potassium iodide and ⅛ teaspoon of cornstarch in 1 ounce of hot water. Filter and save the solution to use as an ink. On the upper half of a sheet of paper, draw a picture. Let dry. Prepare a second ink by diluting 1 part of washable blue ink with 15 parts of water.

✳ Presentation:

Using the second ink, write the name of your picture on the lower half of the paper. Place the paper in a tall glass that contains a small amount of bleach. Add a few drops of dilute hydrochloric acid. DO NOT USE CONCENTRATED ACID. ALWAYS HAVE DILUTE SOLUTIONS PREPARED BY A PERSON WHO IS FAMILIAR WITH HOW ACIDS SHOULD BE HANDLED. Slowly the name of the picture will disappear and the drawing will seem to take its place.

▭ What Happens:

Sodium hypochlorite and hydrochloric acid react to produce chlorine. THE AMOUNT OF CHLORINE PRODUCED IS SAFE TO WORK WITH IN THIS EXPERIMENT. JUST TO BE SAFE, DO NOT INHALE THE VAPORS. The chlorine bleaches the washable blue ink and reacts with the potassium iodide to form iodine. The iodine reacts with the starch to produce a dark, blue-black inklike color picture.

Invisible–Visible–Invisible

In this fourth group, invisible inks are made visible, and then with further treatment, once again invisible.

──────────── (1) ────────────

✔ You Will Need:

Cornstarch; iodine tincture; sodium thiosulfate.

◇ Preparation:

Prepare the following solutions:

No. 1	½ tsp cornstarch in 4 oz boiling water. Let cool and filter off any undissolved starch.
No. 2	1 oz iodine, 2 oz water
No. 3	2 oz sodium thiosulfate 3 oz water

✳ Presentation:

Write a message on paper using the starch. The message is invisible when after the paper dries. When you apply iodine, the writing "magically" appears in a blue-black color. Further treatment with sodium thiosulfate will make the writing invisible.

▭ What Happens:

Iodine reacts with starch to form a blue-black color. Sodium thiosulfate changes it to a colorless, complex iodine-thiosulfate compound.

✔ You Will Need:

Cobalt chloride.

◇ Preparation:

Dissolve ¼ tsp cobalt chloride in 1 ounce of water.

✳ Presentation:

Write a message with the cobalt chloride. Let dry. Heat will develop the writing in a blue-pink to blue color. To make the writing disappear, let it cool or gently blow on it. This demonstration can be repeated.

⟹ What Happens:

When cool, cobalt chloride absorbs moisture from the air and becomes invisible. Heat removes the water, and the cobalt chloride turns blue.

——————————————— (3) ———————————————

✔ You Will Need:

Phenolphthalein solution; sodium carbonate; dilute acetic acid.

◇ Preparation: Wear Goggles

Dissolve 1 teaspoon of sodium carbonate in 2 ounces of water.

✳ Presentation:

Write a message with the phenolphthalein. Let dry. To develop the writing in a red color, lightly blot or spray with sodium carbonate. To make it disappear, apply acetic acid.

⬭ What Happens:

Phenolphthalein, an indicator, turns red with a base (sodium carbonate). Acetic acid neutralizes the sodium carbonate making the surface of the paper acid. In acid, phenolphthalein becomes colorless.

———————————— (4) ————————————

✔ You Will Need:

Phenolphthalein solution; dilute ammonium hydroxide.

◇ Preparation:

Write a message with the phenolphthalein. Let dry and it will become invisible.

✷ Presentation:

Lightly sponge the paper with ammonium hydroxide. Red writing will appear. When exposed to air, the writing will slowly fade and eventually become invisible.

⬭ What Happens:

Phenolphthalein, an indicator, turns red with a base (ammonium hydroxide). When exposed to air, the ammonium hydroxide evaporates and the phenolphthalein turns colorless.

Vanishing Ink

✳ The Effect:

In this effect the magic takes place over a period of several days to a few weeks. It appears as if you can make writing disappear, even when you are miles away and the writing is under lock and key.

✔ You Will Need:

Cornstarch; iodine tincture.

◇ Preparation:

Dissolve ½ teaspoon of starch in 4 ounces of boiling water. Filter off any undissolved starch. Add just enough iodine to turn the solution blue-black. TOO MUCH IODINE WILL PREVENT THE EXPERIMENT FROM WORKING.

✹ Presentation:

Write a message with the iodine-starch solution. Let a member of the audience take it home. Instruct him to place it under lock and key. Over a period of time the writing will vanish.

▭ What Happens:

Exposure to air results in an unstable, colorless iodine-starch compound.

The Pen That Writes White

✳ The Effect:

White writing appears on blue paper.

✔ You Will Need:

Sodium ferrocyanide; ferric ammonium sulfate; sodium carbonate; white bond paper.

◇ Preparation: Wear Gloves

Dissolve the following, each in 3 ounces of water:

No. 1	½ tsp sodium ferrocyanide
	½ tsp ferric ammonium sulfate
No. 2	4 tsp sodium carbonate

Color a sheet of paper blue using solution No. 1. Apply with a soft brush or cotton. Let dry.

✳ Presentation:

Write a message with solution No. 2. White writing will appear.

▭ What Happens:

Chemical reactions produce color changes.

Three Colors From One Pen

✳ The Effect:

You hand a volunteer a sheet of paper, a glass of water, and a pen and ask him to draw a picture. From out of nowhere, his drawing appears in several colors.

✔ You Will Need:

Tannic acid; ferric ammonium sulfate; sodium salicylate; sodium ferrocyanide.

◇ Preparation: Wear Gloves

Mix the following using 1 teaspoon of each chemical:

No. 1	tannic acid and ferric ammonium sulfate
No. 2	sodium salicylate and ferric ammonium sulfate
No. 3	sodium ferrocyanide and ferric ammonium sulfate

Divide a sheet of paper into thirds and rub mixture No. 1 into the top section, mixture No. 2 over the middle section, and mixture No. 3 onto the remaining section. Dust off any excess, trying not to mix the different mixtures.

✳ Presentation:

Write on the paper using water as an ink. The colors black, blue, and red will appear.

⊃ What Happens:

Chemical reactions produce color changes.
SUGGESTIONS:
(1) Try using the chemical combinations from the experiment, *Using Water As A Developer.*
(2) The experiment will work better if finely powdered chemicals are used.

The Question That Answers Itself

✳ The Effect:

I have used this next illustration with great success. I write a question: it disappears, and the answer appears.

✔ You Will Need:

Copper sulfate; dilute ammonium hydroxide; sodium bisulfate.

◇ Preparation: Wear Goggles

Dissolve the following, each in 4 ounces of water:

| No. 1 | ½ tsp copper sulfate, 3 tsp ammonium hydroxide |
| No. 2 | 3 tsp sodium bisulfate |

Select a question that will be asked. You can arrange this with your volunteer in advance. Use solution No. 2 to secretly write the answer on the lower half of a sheet of light blue tinted paper. Let dry.

✴ Presentation:

Write the question with solution No. 1 on the upper half of the paper. Carefully apply low heat. The question will disappear, to be replaced with the answer.

◗ What Happens:

Heat causes ammonium hydroxide to evaporate changing the blue copper hydroxide ink to invisible copper sulfate. The sodium bisulfate produces a dehydration (burning) reaction that resembles black ink.

Another Question That Answers Itself

☀ The Effect:

A variation of the preceding effect.

✔ You Will Need:

Phenolphthalein solution; dilute ammonium hydroxide; sodium bisulfate.

✸ Presentation:

Repeat the last effect, *The Question That Answers Itself,* replacing the blue copper hydroxide ink with one prepared by adding just enough phenolphthalein to 4 teaspoons ammonium hydroxide in 3 ounces of water, in order to turn it red. Carefully apply low heat. The question will disappear, only to be replaced by the answer in dark writing.

▭ What Happens:

Phenolphthalein, an indicator, turns red with a base (ammonium hydroxide). Heat evaporates the ammonium hydroxide causing the phenolphthalein to become colorless. The sodium bisulfate produces a dehydration (burning) reaction that resembles black ink.

CAREFUL

Crazy Question

✳ The Effect:

A question fades away, and slowly an answer appears in its place.

✔ You Will Need:

Sodium ferrocyanide; ferric ammonium sulfate; sodium silicate solution; phenolphthalein solution.

◇ Preparation: Wear Gloves

Using phenolphthalein, write an answer to a previously selected question on the lower half of a sheet of paper and let dry.

✸ Presentation:

Write the question on the upper half of the paper. Use an ink prepared by dissolving ½ teaspoon of sodium ferrocyanide and ½ teaspoon of ferric ammonium sulfate in 4 ounces of water. To make the question vanish and the answer appear, brush a solution of sodium silicate diluted with an equal volume of water over the paper.

▭ What Happens:

Chemical reactions produce color changes.

Mysterious Message I

❋ The Effect:

This trick ends in an unexpected appearance of writing. The paper can be examined before and after without the secret being discovered.

✔ You Will Need:

Sodium bisulfate.

◇ Preparation: Wear Goggles

Write a message on paper with sodium bisulfate (3 teaspoons dissolved in 4 ounces of water). Be sure no one sees you! Use a glass rod or toothpick as a pen. Let dry.

❋ Presentation:

To reveal the writing, carefully heat the paper. The lower the temperature, the slower the message will appear.

▭ What Happens:

Sodium bisulfate produces a dehydration (burning) reaction that resembles black ink.

◆

NEVER TASTE, DRINK, OR SMELL ANY OF THE CHEMICALS OR MIXTURES

Mysterious Message II

✳ The Effect:

A variation of the preceding trick. This time the paper turns black and white writing appears.

✔ You Will Need:

Sodium carbonate; sodium bisulfate.

◇ Preparation: Wear Goggles

Dissolve the following, each in 2 ounces of water.

No. 1	tsp sodium bisulfate
No. 2	8 tsp sodium carbonate

Dampen one side of a sheet of paper with sodium bisulfate. Write a message with the sodium carbonate. Let dry. The paper will appear unprepared.

✳ Presentation:

Gently heat the paper. It will slowly turn black and white writing will appear.

◷ What Happens:

Sodium bisulfate produces a dehydration (burning) reaction that causes the paper to turn black. The sodium carbonate neutralizes the sodium bisulfate in the areas it is applied. As such, a burning reaction does not occur and white writing (color of the paper) appears.

Magic Blotter I

✳ The Effect:

Ghostlike writing appears on untreated paper.

✔ You Will Need:

Ferric ammonium sulfate; potassium ferrocyanide.

◇ Preparation: Wear Gloves

Dissolve the following, each in 3 ounces of water:

No. 1	1 tsp ferric ammonium sulfate
No. 2	1 tsp potassium ferrocyanide

Write a message on white paper with solution No. 1, and let dry.

✳ Presentation:

Moisten a yellow tinted blotter with solution No. 2 and blot the paper to produce blue writing.

⤳ What Happens:

Chemical reactions produce color changes.

Magic Blotter II

✳ The Effect:

This is the same experiment as *Magic Blotter I* but with black writing.

✔ You Will Need:

Tannic acid; ferric ammonium sulfate.

◇ **Preparation:**

Dissolve the following, each in 3 ounces of water:

No. 1   ¾ tsp tannic acid
No. 2   2 tsp ferric ammonium sulfate

Write your message with solution No. 2 on white paper and let it dry.

✳ **Presentation:**

Moisten a yellow tinted blotter with solution No. 2 and blot the paper to produce black writing.

▱ **What Happens:**

Chemical reactions produce color changes.

Magic Blotter III

✳ **The Effect:**

This is a third variation of the same basic experiment, only this time you produce red writing.

✔ **You Will Need:**

Sodium salicylate; ferric ammonium sulfate.

◇ **Preparation:**

Dissolve the following, each in 3 ounces of water:

No. 1   1 tsp sodium salicylate
No. 2   1 tsp ferric ammonium sulfate

Using solution No. 1, write a message on white paper and let it dry.

✳ **Presentation:**

Moisten a yellow tinted blotter with solution No. 2 and blot the paper to produce red writing.

▱ **What Happens:**

Chemical reactions produce color changes.

The Magic Painting

✳ The Effect:

You can paint a picture in vivid colors, using what appears to be water.

✔ You Will Need:

Ferric chloride; potassium thiocyanate; potassium ferrocyanide; tannic acid.

◇ Preparation: Wear Gloves

Lightly outline a picture in pencil on a sheet of paper. In the outlined areas, rub one of the following to produce the color listed.

Potassium thiocyanate	Red
Potassium ferrocyanide	Blue
Tannic acid	Black

Prepare a solution of ferric chloride (2 teaspoons) in water (3 ounces).

✳ Presentation:

Lightly spray the paper with ferric chloride to produce a picture colored red, blue, and black.

Famous Spy Formula

✳ The Effect:

There are many stories told about how this next illusion was first discovered. Whatever the true story, to anyone who doesn't know the secret, it seems like a miracle. Ordinary water causes writing to appear. When the paper dries, the writing vanishes!

✔ You Will Need:

Linseed oil; 10% ammonium hydroxide; light blue blotter.

◇ Preparation:

Mix ½ teaspoon of linseed oil with 5 ounces of ammonium hydroxide. Use to write a message on the blotter and let dry. The writing will be invisible.

✴ Presentation:

Immerse the blotter in water to develop the writing. Remove and let dry and the writing will disappear. The effect can be repeated.

⬭ What Happens:

Linseed oil is soluble in ammonium hydroxide. When it is applied to the blotter, it waterproofs the fibers where they come in contact with the linseed oil. When the paper is placed in water, the oil treated areas remain dry, revealing the writing. When the paper is dry, the writing disappears.

Medicine Cabinet Secret Ink

✳ The Effect:

As with the last experiment, there are many stories also associated with the origin of this invisible ink. One story has it that spies during World War I used it for their undercover activities.

✔ You Will Need:

Aspirin tablets; 95% denatured alcohol; iodine tincture.

◇ Preparation: Wear Goggles

Crush an aspirin tablet and mix with 2 tablespoons of alcohol. Filter and use the liquid as an ink. Let the writing dry.

✹ Presentation:

Heat 2 tablespoons of iodine in a glass pyrex dish. Expose the paper to iodine vapors. Slowly the writing will become visible.

⊃ What Happens:

Certain invisible chemical compounds react with iodine to form visible compounds.

Salt Writing

✳ The Effect:

Rub an ordinary pencil over a sheet of paper to produce a ghostlike message.

✔ You Will Need:

Sodium chloride; water; No. 1 soft lead pencil.

◇ Preparation:

Add 4 ounces of sodium chloride to 8 ounces of boiling water. Let boil for several minutes. Let cool and use the solution as an ink to write a message on paper. After the paper is dry, the writing will be invisible.

✳ Presentation:

Carefully rub a soft lead pencil lightly over the surface of the paper; a message will appear.

▭ What Happens:

Sodium chloride increases the resistance of the paper to the lead pencil.

CAUTION

Photographic Invisible Ink

✸ The Effect:

Show the audience a blank sheet of paper and explain that it is special paper used by haunted spirits. You continue by saying that you can call upon the spirit world and they will respond, causing strange things to happen. As you talk, ghostly writing eerily appears. The paper can be examined afterward without the secret being discovered.

✔ You Will Need:

Silver nitrate.

◇ Preparation: Wear Goggles

Dissolve ¼ teaspoon of silver nitrate in ½ ounce water. Use as an ink and let dry. IMPORTANT! SILVER NITRATE SOLUTION AND THE PREPARED PAPER MUST BE KEPT AWAY FROM LIGHT UNTIL YOU ARE READY FOR YOUR EXPERIMENT.

✷ Presentation:

The paper should be held with the treated side toward a bright light. Depending on how strong the light is, the writing will develop.

⬭ What Happens:

Light changes invisible silver nitrate to visible, nonlight sensitive metallic silver.

Chapter 3

Magic With Ultraviolet Light

In 1801 the German scientist Johann Ritter discovered a band of invisible light radiation that extended beyond the violet end of the visible light spectrum. This light radiation became known as ultraviolet light. Soon it was discovered that there were two types of this radiation - short wave and long wave. Those of us who have had painful sunburns can blame them on too much exposure to the short wave variety.

Unlike the burning properties of short wave ultraviolet radiation, the long wave form is comparatively safe to work with. It can be used in many interesting ways to create unusual effects, especially some that can be adapted for use in stage presentations. Under controlled conditions, ultraviolet light can be used to make the invisible become visible in glowing, vivid colors. It can be used to create light shows and other displays that will long be remembered by those who witness its applications. On the stage, you can present baffling illusions that will make your magic shows truly spectacular. The following experiments are just a few of the many fascinating ways you can use ultraviolet light.

Ultraviolet Light Sources

Ordinary white light contains invisible ultraviolet light radiation in addition to the visible portion of the light spectrum. Using a special filter, the ultraviolet light can be separated from the white light. Another source is the use of self-contained, low wattage lamps that generate ultraviolet light. Both of these sources will produce sufficient light for the experiments in this chapter.

USE ONLY THE LONG WAVE VARIETY. AS A PRECAUTIONARY PROCEDURE, AVOID EXCESSIVE EXPOSURE TO THE LONG WAVE VARIETY.

Filters and ultraviolet light lamps, as well as other accessories and supplies can be found by writing to the sources listed in *Where to Get Chemicals and Equipment for Ultraviolet Light Experiments*. You can also check art supply stores, arts and crafts stores, science equipment companies, hobby shops, and school science laboratories.

How Florescence Is Produced

Some substances have atoms that absorb energy when exposed to ultraviolet light. When this occurs, electrons in the atomic structure of these materials become agitated and attempt to eliminate this energy. Release of this energy produces fluorescence. When you turn off the ultraviolet light, the electron activity stops and the fluorescence ends.

Invisible Light Paint

✳ The Effect:

Objects glow with a weird, ghostlike color when exposed to ultraviolet light.

✔ You Will Need:

Fluorescein sodium; 5% sodium carbonate solution; gum arabic; distilled water.

◇ Preparation:

Mix 2 teaspoons of gum arabic with 2 ounces of hot water. Let stand for 24 to 48 hours until dissolved. Strain off any lumps. Dissolve 2 teaspoons of fluorescein in 2 ounces of sodium carbonate and add 1 ounce of gum arabic. Shake to mix and store in a tightly sealed bottle.

✱ Presentation:

Use as a paint and apply to different objects. When dry the paint will be invisible. Exposure to ultraviolet light will produce a weird, ghostlike color (fluorescence).

⬭ What Happens:

See *How Fluorescence Is Produced.*

Flourescent Paints

✳ The Effect:

The following mixtures will transform objects into eerie, phantomlike pieces of art when exposed to ultraviolet light.

✔ You Will Need:

See following formulas.

◇ Preparation:

Green Fluorescent Paint

Mix 4 tablespoons of luminous calcium sulfide, 4 teaspoons prepared barium sulfate and 4 teaspoons of green chromic oxide. Combine with 3 ounces of spar varnish.

Blue Fluorescent Paint

Mix 2 teaspoons of prepared barium sulfate, 1 teaspoon of ultramarine blue and 10 teaspoons of luminous calcium sulfide. Combine with linseed oil, mixing to make a smooth consistency.

Orange Fluorescent Paint

Combine 7 teaspoons of prepared barium sulfate, ½ teaspoon of prepared India yellow, ¾ teaspoon of prepared madder lake and 14 teaspoons of luminous calcium sulfide. Mix with thin spar varnish.

Red Fluorescent Paint

Dissolve ½ gram of rhodamine-B in 1 teaspoon of 95% denatured alcohol. Mix with 4 ounces of clear lacquer. To deepen the color, increase the rhodamine-B.

Yellow Fluorescent Paint

Dissolve ⅛ gram of eosin and ⅛ gram of fluorescein in 2 teaspoons of 95% denatured alcohol. Mix with 4 ounces of clear lacquer.

✳ Presentation:

Use as paints and apply to different objects. Several colors can be applied to the same object. Let dry and expose to ultraviolet light to produce a spooky effect in vivid colors.

▭ What Happens:

See *How Fluorescence Is Produced.*

Ghosts

✳ The Effect:

Easy to perform, the audience will be amazed as you make contact with the spirit world. You can command ghosts to appear and disappear as you wish.

✔ You Will Need:

Quinine sulfate; 10% sodium bisulfate solution; gum arabic; distilled water.

◇ Preparation: Wear Goggles

Mix 2 teaspoons of gum arabic with 2 ounces of hot water. Let stand for 24 to 48 hours until dissolved. Strain off any lumps. Dissolve 2 teaspoons of sodium bisulfate in 1 ounce of water. Combine with ½ ounce of gum arabic and add with stirring 1 tablespoon of quinine sulfate.

✳ Presentation:

Shake well before using. Secretly paint a picture of a ghost on an artist's canvas and let dry. To make the ghost appear, expose the canvas to ultraviolet light. Turn the light off and the ghost will disappear. To make the effect more mysterious, hide the light and arrange for it to be turned on very slowly.

▭ What Happens:

See *How Fluorescence Is Produced.*

Ghostly Spirits

✳ The Effect:

On an empty stage, or in a locked room, a ghost materializes and then disappears. Volunteers can guard the doors and windows to make certain that you, as the magician, are not using any assistants.

✔ You Will Need:

White petroleum jelly.

◇ Preparation:

Secretly apply petroleum jelly lightly to your face (around your eyes and mouth, and down to the bridge of your nose).

✴ Presentation:

Darken the room and turn on the ultraviolet light. You will suddenly vanish and be replaced by an apparition. Turn off the light and the apparition will vanish. Turn on the room lights and you reappear.

⌁ What Happens:

See *How Fluorescence Is Produced.*

◆

NEVER TASTE, DRINK, OR SMELL ANY OF THE CHEMICALS OR MIXTURES

More Ghostly Spirits

✳ The Effect:

This is an excellent illusion to combine with the last experiment, *Ghostly Spirit.* The stage is darkened, you disappear, and a ghost appears in blazing color.

✔ You Will Need:

Fluorescein sodium; distilled water.

◇ Preparation:

Soak your clothes in a 2% fluorescein sodium solution. Let dry and get dressed. Darken the stage and turn on the ultraviolet light. You will disappear, to be replaced by a ghostlike apparition. Turn off the ultraviolet light, the ghost will vanish, and you will reappear.

▭ What Happens:

See *How Fluorescence Is Produced.*

Ultraviolet Light Accessories

There are many accessories you can use to transform ordinary objects into brightly glowing fluorescent pieces. When treated and allowed to dry, the preparation is invisible. Exposure to ultraviolet light will turn them into fascinating and bewildering objects that can be used in stage productions, at parties, as decorations, and more. For information on how ultraviolet light can be produced, see *Ultraviolet Light Sources*.

Ultraviolet Light Spray

This is a pressurized spray of a fluorescing mixture that will transform objects into eerie items when exposed to ultraviolet light. It glows with a blue-white color and dry cleaning fluid will remove it.

Chalk

Available in several colors, this chalk can be used the same way as ordinary chalk. It will glow with vivid colors when exposed to ultraviolet light.

Invisible Ink

Generally supplied as a rubber stamp pad, it is usually used to identify individuals who enter and leave a room. Invisible when dry, it glows with a pale light when exposed to ultraviolet light. Soap and water will wash it off.

Tempera Paint

Fluorescent tempera paints are valuable adjuncts to ultraviolet light experiments. Water base paints come in several colors and are widely used for making posters, decorations, or stage settings.

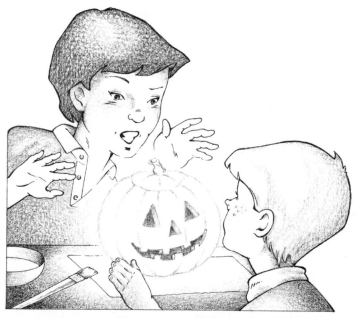

Ultraviolet Light Projects

Fluorescent Pottery

Pottery and other stone arrangements can be treated with fluorescing materials and when exposed to ultraviolet light will create new dimensions in design and unusual colors.

Hypnotic Bands of Color

Rapidly revolving disks (thin plywood or heavy cardboard) decorated with fluorescent paints (several colors can be used at the same time) become almost hypnotic displays of unusual colors when rapidly revolved and exposed to ultraviolet light. An electric or hand drill can be used to make the disks revolve.

Black Light Bubbles

Place a bubble making machine inside a plastic dome. Include a source of ultraviolet light. Add 2% fluorescein sodium solution to the soap bubble mixture. Load the bubble machine and turn it on. The bubbles will glow with vivid, blazing color as they are produced.

Stage Magic

Ultraviolet light can be used in theatrical productions to create unusual costumes and settings. Props and scenery painted with fluorescent paints (see *Ultraviolet Light Accessories, Tempera Paint*) and costumes treated with fluorescein sodium (see *More Ghostly Spirits*) will be dramatically different from those normally used.

A Ghostly Show

✳ The Effect:

You have been introduced to the basics of fluorescence. Now you can put it all together in this next illusion. The stage is empty...the lights slowly dim...the stage becomes dark...music sets the mood (Massenet's Elegie is excellent background music). Out of thin air apparitions appear, ghosts materialize, a skeleton changes to three dancing skeletons and more...and then everything vanishes. The lights come on and the stage is empty. The audience marvels at your ability to call upon the deepest realms of ghostly mysteries.

◇ Preparation:

Construct the following:

Bell

• Cut a bell-shaped form approximately 24 inches high, also a clapper, from ¼″ plywood or heavy cardboard. Sand smooth and apply two coats of fluorescent paint. Paint ½ inch stripes of dull black paint around the edges. Also paint the back. Fasten the clapper loosely so that it will swing back and forth.

Ghostly Heads

• Paint a picture of a person's head on a fan at least 24 inches wide when open. The area around the picture, the handle, and back should be painted a dull black.

Skeletons

• These are the kind usually sold at Halloween. They should be at least 5 feet tall and constructed so they can be taken apart. Take them apart and treat one side with black light spray (see *Ultraviolet Light Accessories*) or with a 2% solution of fluorescein sodium (see *More Ghostly Spirits*). Paint the backs a dull black. Reassemble.

Ghostly Forms

• Use muslin at least 5 to 6 feet long and 24 inches wide. Treat with a 2% fluorescein sodium solution (see *More Ghostly Spirits*). Tie the muslin to a long, thin pole painted a dull black. Use strong, black nylon thread. The distance between the pole and muslin should not be longer than six inches.

Trumpet
• Paint a trumpet with fluorescent tempera paint (see *Ultraviolet Light Accessories*). Suspend from a long pole painted a dull black. Use two pieces of strong black nylon thread, a piece at each end of the trumpet.

Ghostly Light on the Magician
• Cover the lens of a flashlight with green cellophane. The barrel of the flashlight should be painted dull black.

Stage Costumes
• Cut and sew shrouds from muslin dyed dull black. Make small holes for breathing and seeing.

Ultraviolet Light
• This can be a single flood light with an ultraviolet light filter, or ultraviolet light bulb. It is important that the light is strong enough to flood the entire stage.

✳ Presentation:

With the house lights on, you walk on stage secretly carrying the flashlight. Begin by saying, "Ladies and gentlemen, throughout the centuries of time much has been written about ghosts and their sudden, mysterious, and unexplainable appearances. It has always been a popular pastime for people of all ages to tell ghost stories. Many of you have witnessed supernatural happenings. There are some of you, I'm sure, who claim not to believe in ghosts yet are afraid to explore a haunted house. Tonight I ask that all of you - believers and nonbelievers - concentrate on what you will witness on this stage, and then ask yourselves if ghosts exist."

Off stage an assistant dims the lights and turns on the background music. A gong sounds, the stage turns completely dark, chains are heard rattling along with the sound of wind. For an added effect, assistants in the balconies can drop a few kernels of rice on the audience below. You shine the flashlight on your face and ask your audience to be completely still. Any noise, you explain, might scare away the spirits.

The gong sounds again, cueing you to turn off your flashlight. It is now completely dark and you say, "I feel the presence of friendly spirits among us." Your assistant turns on the ultraviolet light. Suddenly a large bell appears and your audience hears a loud clanging. It vanishes, only to appear somewhere else. This illusion is done by one of your assistants who is dressed in black. He carries the bell, black side toward the audience and, upon his cue, reverses the bell so that the fluorescent side is exposed to the ultraviolet light.

The bell vanishes (reversed and carried off stage) and is replaced by an assistant, also dressed in black, who carries the three skeletons held together as one. Turning the fluorescent paint treated side to the ultraviolet light, the skeleton multiplies into three as they are handed to other assistants. As they dance about the stage, chains are heard rattling. The skeletons then vanish, one at a time, as they are turned around and carried off stage.

Next the ghostly faces appear and disappear as assistants open and close the fans. This creates an illusion of ectoplasmic materialization and will be more effective if done slowly. Finally the ghostly forms and trumpets are produced by assistants who manipulate the poles to which they are tied. After being removed from the stage, the ultraviolet light is turned off and the house lights come up. The stage is empty. Only you remain! From the looks of amazement on the faces of the people in your audience, you can tell that you now have more believers in ghostly doings than before.

Chapter 4

Chemical Magic With Time

The stage lights dim and a spotlight keys in on the magician and an assistant from the audience. The magician hands him a glass and fills it with water. Standing away to ensure no physical or mechanical contact, he asks his assistant to concentrate on ink.

After a few seconds of concentration, the water in the glass suddenly changes to ink! With everyone wondering how it was accomplished, there will be no doubt in the minds of the audience that this is an outstanding display of magic. I will tell you how it was done in

this chapter and give you other, similar, illusions. Remember, these are some of the most bewildering and mindboggling illusions in the repertoire of magic and will certainly hold your audiences spellbound as you entertain them with magical mysteries for which there appears to be no explanation.

IMPORTANT— READ FIRST

• Some of the experiments require dilute sulfuric acid. Although the dilute acid is safe to work with, as a precaution, take extra care when you are using it. DO NOT USE CONCENTRATED ACID. ALWAYS HAVE DILUTE SOLUTIONS PREPARED BY A PERSON WHO IS FAMILIAR WITH HOW ACIDS SHOULD BE HANDLED. In case of an accidental spill, neutralize the acid with a strong solution of baking soda (sodium bicarbonate) and wash with large amounts of cool water.
• Always use freshly prepared solutions that are not over two days old, and have been kept in airtight, dark glass bottles.

Think Ink

✳ The Effect:

Mixing two glasses of water, the water suddenly changes to ink.

✔ You Will Need:

Potassium iodate; cornstarch; anhydrous sodium sulfite; 0.5% sulfuric acid; distilled water.

◇ Preparation:

Prepare the following solutions:

No. 1   2 grams potassium iodate in 500 ml water.

No. 2   1 gram cornstarch in 50 ml water. Warm to dissolve. Filter and cool. Add ¼ gram sodium sulfite and sulfuric acid to make 500 ml.

✳ Presentation:

Pour 2 ounces of solution No. 1 into a glass containing 2 ounces of solution No. 2. After a few seconds the water will suddenly change to a dark blue ink-like color.

▭ What Happens:

- Solutions 1 and 2 react to form sulfurous and iodic acids.
- Sulfurous and iodic acids react to form hydriodic and sulfurous acids.
- Hydriodic acid reacts with excess sulfurous acid to form iodine.
- Iodine reacts with the sulfurous acid to form hydriodic acid.
- The above reactions continue until all the sulfurous acid has reacted and the iodine is in excess.
- The excess iodine reacts with the starch to produce a dark blue color.

Colored Clock Reaction -Red

✳ The Effect:

Water changes to a red colored liquid.

✔ You Will Need:

Sodium metabisulfite; anhydrous sodium sulfite; 35 to 40% formalin solution; phenolphthalein solution; distilled water.

◇ Preparation: Wear Goggles

Prepare the following solutions:

No. 1   5 grams sodium metabisulfite and ¾ gram sodium sulfite in 250 ml water. Add 1 ml phenolphthalein.

No. 2   25 ml formalin diluted with water to make 250 ml.

✱ Presentation:

Pour 2 ounces of solution No. 2 into a glass containing 2 ounces of solution No. 1. In a few seconds the water will suddenly change to a red liquid.

⬭ What Happens:

• Phenolphthalein, an indicator, turns red with a base and colorless in acids (sodium metabisulfite and sodium sulfite).
• Formalin reacts with sodium metabisulfite and sodium sulfite to form sodium hydroxide (base).
• A secondary reaction takes place in which excess sodium sulfite neutralizes the sodium hydroxide. This continues until all the sulfite is used up and the solution becomes basic, and the phenolphthalein turns red.

SUGGESTION: If the color change is too slow, increase the formalin or decrease the sodium sulfite. If too fast, decrease the formalin or increase the sodium sulfite.

※

✔

◇

※

▭

Colored Clock Reaction - Blue

Repeat the last experiment, substituting 2 ml thymolphthalein solution (¼ gram dissolved in 25 ml 95% denatured alcohol) for the phenolphthalein.

Reversal

※ The Effect:

Pour one of the colored solutions from the experiments COLORED CLOCK REACTION - RED, COLORED CLOCK REACTION - BLUE into an empty glass. Mysteriously they change to water.

✔ You Will Need:

Sodium bisulfite.

◇ Preparation:

Dissolve 3 teaspoons of sodium bisulfite in as little water as possible. Pour it into a glass.

※ Presentation:

Pour one of the colored solutions into the glass containing the sodium bisulfite. The solution will turn to water.

▭ What Happens:

Thymolphthalein and phenolphthalein are indicators, and are colorless with an acid (sodium bisulfite).

Many Colors

✳ The Effect:

Water poured into a glass changes color, from yellow to deep purple, to red, and finally yellow-green.

✔ You Will Need:

Sodium thiosulfate; ferric chloride; distilled water.

◇ Preparation:

Prepare the following solutions.

No. 1	2.5 grams sodium thiosulfate in 100 ml water.
No. 2	1.6 grams ferric chloride in 100 ml water.

✸ Presentation:

Pour solution No. 1, with stirring, into a glass containing solution No. 2. The yellow color will mysteriously turn deep purple, then red, and finally yellow-green.

▭ What Happens:

Ferric chloride and sodium thiosulfate react progressively to form complex compounds that have different colors.

Many Colors Improved

✳ The Effect:

The preceding experiment repeated with a variation that makes it more mystifying.

✔ You Will Need:

Sodium thiosulfate; ferric chloride; distilled water.

◇ Preparation:

Prepare the following solutions:

No. 1   3.2 grams ferric chloride in 20 ml water.

No. 2   5 grams sodium thiosulfate in 20 ml water.

Prepare a glass with 2 ml of solution No. 1. Dilute 2 ml of solution No. 2 with 400 ml of water.

✳ Presentation:

Pour solution No. 2 into the glass containing solution No. 1. The water will turn deep purple, then red, and finally yellow-green.

⟹ What Happens:

Ferric chloride and sodium thiosulfate react progressively to form complex compounds that have different colors.

Chapter 5

Cold Light Chemical Magic

Just a little over two centuries ago, magicians were amazing their audiences with a different kind of magic – chemical magic. Some people believed that magicians were in league with the devil who gave them special powers to perform their miraculous illusions. Today audiences are still amazed at what you can do with chemical magic but they know that the illusions are the results of simple, explainable chemical principles and not because of supernatural powers. As a result of twentieth century discoveries in chemistry, magicians are able to design sophisticated and bewildering illusions. The secrets you will learn in this chapter come from one of these modern discoveries. I have adapted these secrets into illusions that are sure to change your ordinary magic routines into stage shows that your audiences will remember long after the lights have dimmed and the curtains closed.

What Cold Light Is

Cold light was discovered in 1912 but it was not until 25 years later that an accidental discovery revealed the chemiluminescent (cold light) producing properties of luminol (3- aminophthalhydrazide). Scientists at the Massachusetts Institute of Technology discovered that this molecular arrangement of carbon, hydrogen, oxygen, and nitrogen, when used in combination with other chemical compounds will produce cold light (also described as light without heat). They found that an alkaline solution of luminol mixed with an oxygen producing compound (hydrogen peroxide) and an oxygen releasing compound (potassium ferrocyanide) will react to produce cold light that is strong enough to read by. Understanding how chemiluminescence works led to the discovery of other chemical combinations that will produce cold light.

IMPORTANT - READ FIRST

• Do not use lumi*nal* (sodium-5-ethyl-5-phenyl bar-biturate) that can be obtained only by prescription from a drugstore. IT IS NOT THE SAME as lumi*nol* (3-aminophthalhydrazide) that will have to be purchased from chemical supply companies.

• Always use freshly prepared solutions that are not over two days old, and have been kept in airtight, dark glass bottles.

Wear Goggles and Gloves
When Preparing All the Experiments
In This Section.

Chemiluminescence

✳ The Effect:

Mixing two liquids causes a mysterious light to appear.

✔ You Will Need:

Prepare the following solutions:

No. 1   0.2 gram luminol in 20 ml
sodium hydroxide. Dilute
with water to make 2000 ml.

No. 2   0.5 gram potassium
ferricyanide in 50 ml water.
Add 20 ml hydrogen peroxide
and dilute with water to
make 2000 ml.

✳ Presentation:

Darken the room. Pour both solutions at the same time into
a large jar. As they mix, chemiluminescence is produced.
Adding small amounts of potassium ferricyanide will
increase and prolong the production of cold light.

⬭ What Happens:

See *What Cold Light Is.*

Colored Chemiluminescence

✳ The Effect:

Chemiluminescence can be made more vivid by the addition of dye.

◇ Preparation:

Prepare the following solution:

Sodium hydroxide	1 gram
Water (to make)	2000 ml
Luminol	¼ gram
Dye	0.1 to 0.2 gram
Hydrogen peroxide	50 ml

Dissolve the chemicals in the order listed.

✳ Presentation:

Pour the solution into a tall, cylindrical glass container. Darken the room. Drop in potassium ferricyanide crystals. Colored streams of chemiluminescence appear. The dyes that can be used include:

Dye	Color
Fluorescein sodium	Yellow-green
Rhodamine-B	Light rose
Eosine yellow	Pink
Rhodamine-B and Fluorescein sodium (equal amounts)	Orange
Erythrosine B	Lavender

▭ What Happens:

See *What Cold Light Is*. The dyes are additive compounds that do not react with the other ingredients. Their purpose is only to add color to the solutions.

Magic Lamp

✳ The Effect:

An eerie red light appears when two solutions are mixed.

✔ You Will Need:

35 to 40% formalin solution; 5% pyrogallol solution (freshly prepared; 3% hydrogen peroxide; 10% sodium carbonate solution.

◇ Preparation:

Prepare the following solution:

Formalin	3 ounces
Pyrogallol	3 ounces
Sodium carbonate	3 ounces

✳ Presentation:

In a darkened room pour the solution into a glass jar. Add 3 ounces of hydrogen peroxide. A deep red light will appear.

▭ What Happens:

Oxygen from the hydrogen peroxide reacts with the other ingredients to produce red chemiluminescence.

83

Floating Lights

✳ The Effect:

Weird lights appear floating on the surface of a liquid.

✔ You Will Need:

Luminol; sodium hydroxide; 3% hydrogen peroxide; potassium ferricyanide crystals; distilled water; white blotting paper.

◇ Preparation:

Prepare the following solution:

Sodium hydroxide	½ gram
Water (to make)	1000 ml
Luminol	⅛ gram
Hydrogen peroxide	25 ml

Dissolve the chemicals in the order listed.

✳ Presentation:

Pour the solution into a wide glass dish. Float small squares of blotting paper on the surface of the solution. Darken the room and drop a few potassium ferrocyanide crystals on each piece of paper. Blazing, islands of light spring forth.

▭ What Happens:

See *What Cold Light Is*.

✳

✔

◇

✶

▭

**Wear Goggles and Gloves
When Preparing All the Experiments
In This Section.**

Chapter 6

Creative Crafts Magic

With this chapter we depart a little from the usual chemical experiments and move into the wonderful world of fascinating and unusual art forms, and craft projects. Here we take everyday chemicals and transform them into new things with special uses. You will learn how to make modeling and casting mediums, pastes and glues, paints, papier mache, and much, much more. For example, flour, sawdust, plaster of Paris, and water will make an easy-to-work-with medium for hundreds of uses. Or, stirring together cornstarch, salt, water, and a few drops of food color will create a simple paint. Like many of the experiments in the earlier chapters, these also use inexpensive materials you can get from grocery stores, variety stores, or hardware stores. A few, however, are specialized items that you can buy from art supply stores or craft and hobby dealers.

I have also included suggestions on how some of these concoctions can be used with other materials to make exciting crafts objects. Best of all, these experiments are fun to do and will give you many opportunities to use your creativity.

Modeling Mediums

Sand and Sawdust Mixtures

(1)

✔ You Will Need:
Sawdust; dry wallpaper paste; water.

◇ Preparation:
Mix 4 cups of sawdust and 1 cup of wallpaper paste with water to make a thick doughlike mixture. This modeling medium can be prepared a day or two in advance, and will remain soft if kept covered with a damp cloth. Store in a cool place. Objects made from this medium should be air dried at room temperature.

SUGGESTION: The addition of 1 cup of plaster of Paris (increase the water if necessary) will add weight to the mixture. You can make book ends, door stops, paperweights - almost anything that requires weight. The plaster of Paris limits the mixture's keeping properties so use it within 30 to 45 minutes.

(2)

✔ You Will Need:
Sawdust; liquid white glue.

◇ Preparation:
Mix sawdust with glue to make a doughlike mixture that can be modeled. This medium cannot be stored but must be used immediately. Air dry at room temperature. Dried objects can be sandpapered and sprayed with shellac or lacquer, or painted.

(3)

✔ You Will Need:

Sawdust; nonrising flour; salt; water.

◇ Preparation:

Combine 2 cups of sawdust, 1 cup of flour, and 1 teaspoon of salt with water to make a doughlike mixture that will hold its shape without cracking. Add more sawdust if too thin. Air dry objects at room temperature.

(4)

✔ You Will Need:

Sawdust; plaster of Paris; white lead; litharge; liquid white glue.

◇ Preparation:

Combine 1 cup of sawdust, 5 cups of plaster of Paris, 4 cups of white lead, and 1 cup of litharge with glue to make a stiff mixture that can be worked with modeling tools. This medium cannot be stored. Use as soon as prepared. It will air dry to a hard finish.
SUGGESTION: When you increase the glue, you get a thick paste that can be applied with a stiff brush.

(5)

✔ You Will Need:

Sawdust; cornstarch; water.

◇ Preparation:

Mix 2 ounces of cornstarch with 3 cups of water. Stir to make a smooth mixture. Cook over low heat, stirring until a smooth, pastelike texture forms. Let cool. Add, in small amounts, 2 to 4 cups of sawdust. Knead until mixed. The mixture should be wet enough to hold its shape without cracking when worked with. Air dry objects at room temperature.

Notes

(6)

✔ You Will Need:

Washed sand; cornstarch; powdered alum; water.

◇ Preparation:

Combine 2 cups of sand, 1 cup of cornstarch and 2 teaspoons of alum with water, stirring until mixed. You can make a colored medium by adding a few drops of food color. Cook over low heat, stirring constantly, until the mixture thickens. Let cool before using. If stored in air tight jars, this craft concoction will keep for several days. Air dry objects at room temperature.

Cornstarch and Flour Mixtures

(1)

✔ You Will Need:

Nonrising flour; salt; olive oil; water.

◇ Preparation:

Combine 1 cup of salt, 2 cups of flour, and 2 tablespoons of olive oil with water. Knead to make a soft, non-sticky dough that will hold its shape without cracking. To make a colored dough, add a few drops of food coloring when kneading. Articles made from this medium can be air dried in a warm place. For a harder finish, bake in an oven at 200 degrees. Check every few minutes to prevent burning. Apply a sealer coat of shellac or lacquer to dried articles.

(2)

✔ You Will Need:

Nonrising flour; salt; cream of tartar; corn oil; water.

◇ Preparation:

Mix 3 cups of flour, 1 cup of salt, and 6 teaspoons of cream of tartar. Blend with 2 cups of boiling water and 6 teaspoons of corn oil. Let cool and knead to form a smooth doughlike texture. If too stiff, add more water. If stored in a tightly covered glass jar, it will keep for several months without refrigeration. This modeling medium will air dry to a hard finish. Apply a sealer coat of lacquer to dried articles.

(3)

✔ You Will Need:

Cornstarch; salt; corn oil; water.

◇ Preparation:

Make a smooth paste of 1 cup of cornstarch and ½ cup of warm water. Mix 2 cups of salt with 1 cup of boiling water and combine with cornstarch. Add 1 teaspoon of corn oil. Cook over low heat, stirring to make a thick, doughlike mixture. Let cool. Knead until it forms a smooth consistency. Articles made from this craft medium can be dried in an oven at 200 degrees, or by exposing to warm air for at least one week. Shellac or spray with lacquer when dry.

Paper Modeling Mixtures

(1)

✔ You Will Need:

Tissue paper; dry wallpaper paste; water.

◇ Preparation:

Soak small pieces of tissue paper in water overnight. Drain off the water and add wallpaper paste to make a mixture that can be modeled.

(2)

✔ You Will Need:

Crepe paper; salt; nonrising flour; water.

◇ Preparation:

Combine ½ cup of flour and ½ cup of salt with water to make a thick, creamlike mixture. Add shredded crepe paper, stirring and kneading to make a mixture that will hold its shape when you work with it.

(3)

See Papier Mache; Papier Mache Strips; Papier Mache Mash.

Tips on Working with Modeling Mixtures

• Make small amounts of modeling mixtures since they tend to dry out quickly.

• The smooth texture of cornstarch and flour mixtures makes them excellent for making intricate figures. You can create mobiles and hanging decorations by rolling the dough flat and cutting with cookie cutters or a knife dipped in water.

• Cornstarch and flour mixtures can be used in place of clay when using molds. Lubricate the mold with petroleum jelly. Do not let dry by baking. Let stand in warm air.

• Modeling mixtures that contain sawdust or sand dry grainy and appear almost stonelike. They are excellent for making sculptures, bookends, door stops, paper weights, etc. Sandpaper smooth and finish with shellac, varnish, lacquer, or plastic sealer.

• Pieces made from modeling mixture that contain glue can be fastened together by moistening with water and applying gentle pressure.

• To add color, blend a few drops of food color or other water soluble dye to the dough and knead until blended.

• You can add decorations to moist articles by applying pressure and letting dry. Fasten with glue on dried objects.

• Smooth articles that have dried can be given a porcelainlike finish by painting with 3 or 4 coats of liquid white glue. Dilute the glue with an equal volume of water.

Rising Concoction

✔ You Will Need:

Sugar; yeast; all-purpose flour; cooking oil; water; salt.

◇ Preparation:

Dissolve 3 tablespoons of sugar in 2 cups of lukewarm water. Stir in the yeast and let stand for 5 minutes. Combine 7 cups of flour, 2 teaspoons of salt and 2 ounces of oil, and add in small amounts to the sugar/water solution, mixing to make a smooth, non- sticky dough. Add more flour if necessary.

How To Use

Roll the dough flat on a floured surface. Cut out different shapes using cookie cutters or a knife dipped in water. Individual pieces can be joined by moistening with water and applying slight pressure. Place on a cookie sheet and let stand in a warm place for 15 to 20 minutes to rise. Decorations can be added before they rise. Bake in an oven at 350 degrees. Let cool and seal with shellac.

Modeling Concoction

✔ You Will Need:

Salt; nonrising flour; sawdust; calcimine paint; water.

◇ Preparation:

Combine ½ cup of salt and 1 cup of flour with water to make a thick paste. Add sawdust that has been colored by mixing with calcimine paint. The finished mixture should have a thick creamlike consistency. Add more water if needed.

How To Use:

Outline on heavy cardboard or thin plywood a picture or design that will be filled using Modeling Concoction. Fill each section, one color at a time, letting it dry before working with the next color. To build up thick areas, use cardboard strips as a form. Remove when the mixture has set up enough to hold its shape. (See *Salt Paint, Modeling Paint.*)

Plastic Wood Dough

Preparing the Wood Dough

✔ You Will Need:

Celluloid; acetone; 95% denatured alcohol; castor oil;
sawdust; oil soluble dye.

◇ Preparation: Wear Goggles

A popular craft material, similar to several commercial
products, can be prepared by dissolving 20 grams of
celluloid in a mixture of 3 ounces of acetone, 3 ounces of
95% denatured alcohol and 2 teaspoons of castor oil.
CAUTION: EXTINGUISH ALL FLAMES. ACETONE AND
ALCOHOL ARE INFLAMMABLE. To add color, dissolve a
small amount of oil soluble dye in the acetone/alcohol/castor
oil before combining with the celluloid. Occasional stirring
will help dissolve the celluloid. Use a glass or wood stirring
rod. To prevent evaporation, keep the mixture in a GLASS
JAR WITH A METAL COVER. DO NOT USE A PLASTIC
CONTAINER OR COVER. If the final mixture is too thin,
increase the celluloid; too thick, add more alcohol. It should
have a thick creamlike consistency. Add sawdust in small
amounts. The wood dough should be moist enough to hold
together without cracking when used. Store in tightly
covered glass or metal containers.

Notes

Using Plastic Wood Dough

✔ You Will Need:

Nonhardening modeling clay; plastic wood dough; plaster of Paris; water.

◇ Preparation:

Making a plaster mold:

1. Using clay, sculpture a model of the object to be cast.

2. Mix the plaster of Paris with water, making a thick, creamlike suspension (see *How To Make Plaster Castings*.)

3. Pour the plaster over the clay to a thickness of approximately ½ inch. Let harden.

4. Carefully remove the clay sculpture. Do not try to save it.

5. Let the mold dry for at least one week.

Making a copy:

1. Soak the mold in water. Remove. With wet hands press the dough into the mold to a thickness of approximately ¼ inch, thicker for large castings. Fill small details by pressing with a toothpick.

2. Immerse in water and leave for 12 hours.

3. Remove from the water, blot dry and carefully chip away the mold.

4. Let the plastic wood dough copy dry for several days.

5. Sand smooth and finish with paint, shellac, or wax.

Bread Dough

✔ You Will Need:

White bread (remove crusts); liquid white glue; food colors.

◇ Preparation:

For each slice of bread add a mixture of 1 teaspoon each of glue and water. Knead to form a smooth dough that is not sticky. If necessary, increase the glue and water, or use more bread. To add color, knead a few drops of food color with the dough. This modeling medium will keep for several days if kept in tightly capped jars. It will dry overnight when exposed to air, or by baking for 3 to 4 hours in an oven at 250 degrees, longer for larger objects. Be sure you check it frequently to prevent burning. Let cool and seal with shellac.

◆

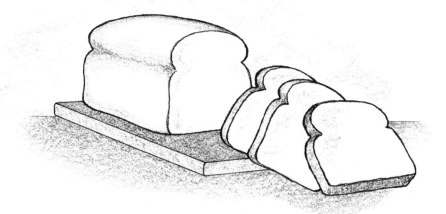

*

✔

◇

Baker's Clay

✔ You Will Need:

Nonrising flour; salt; water.

◇ Preparation:

Knead 4 cups of flour and 1 cup of salt with water to make a heavy dough. Mold with your hands or roll flat and cut different shapes. Decorations can be added (sequins, buttons, shells, etc.). Bake in an oven at 350 degrees. The time will vary with the size of the object. Let cool and seal with shellac.

◆

How To Make A Mold I

✔ You Will Need:

Olive oil; sifted cornstarch; beeswax; petroleum jelly.

◇ Preparation:

Over low heat, melt 8 ounces of beeswax and 2 ounces of olive oil. Add, in small amounts, approximately 8 ounces of cornstarch. Mix and heat until the mixture thickens. Let cool. The mixture will harden.

HOW TO USE:

Set the oven on low heat (not over 200 degrees) and soften the mixture. Coat the object to be duplicated with petroleum jelly and cover with the molding mixture. Let harden. Carefully separate the mold from the object. You might have to tap it gently.

*

◁

How To Make A Mold II

✔ You Will Need:

Dry glue; litharge; white lead; plaster of Paris; sawdust; water.

◇ Preparation: Wear Goggles

Prepare the following mixture:

Litharge	8 ounces
White lead	16 ounces
Plaster of Paris	20 ounces
Sawdust	2 ounces

Dissolve 20 ounces of glue in 64 ounces of hot water and strain. Add the glue, in small amounts, to the dry mixture until a smooth, puttylike mass forms.

HOW TO USE:

Coat the object to be duplicated with petroleum jelly. Cover with the molding mixture and let harden. Carefully separate the mold from the object. Let dry for one week before using.

Commercial Molds

Many arts and crafts stores, as well as hobby shops, sell ready-to-use molds and mold making materials. The more popular types include flexible and nonflexible plastic molds, metal molds, and easy-to-use latex molds.

How To Make Plaster Castings

✔ You Will Need:

Plaster of Paris; petroleum jelly; liquid white glue; water; molds.

◇ Preparation:

Mix plaster of Paris (3 parts by volume) with water (2 parts by volume) to make a thick, creamlike suspension. Add the plaster to the water. Let stand without stirring for 3 for 4 minutes. Then stir slowly to prevent air bubbles from forming. Air bubbles will weaken plaster of Paris castings. Let stand another few minutes. You can make smoother castings by adding 1 ounce of glue to each quart of water before mixing with the plaster of Paris.

HOW TO USE:

Coat the mold (see *How To Make A Mold I; How To Make A Mold II; Commercial Molds*) with petroleum jelly. Fill with the plaster just up to slightly below the edge of the mold. Tap lightly to dislodge any air bubbles that may have formed. Finish filling the mold and set aside to harden. HANDLE WITH CARE. THE PLASTER WILL BECOME HOT TO THE TOUCH. Let cool. When hard, carefully separate the mold from the casting. Gentle tapping may be necessary. Let the copy dry for one week before finishing (see *Professional Casting Techniques*).

Professional Casting Techniques

Adding Texture

Texturizing will produce unusual surface patterns. Try mixing ground coffee with the plaster before pouring. Other materials include vermiculite, sand, small stones, feathers, shredded cloth, etc.

Sanding

Plaster of Paris castings can be sanded using No. 400 wet or dry sandpaper. Do not use too much pressure when sanding.

Curing

Curing is the process of letting plaster of Paris castings harden. It can be speeded up by baking in an oven set at its LOWEST TEMPERATURE, for not longer than 3 to 4 hours.

Sealing

To prevent plaster of Paris castings from absorbing finishing coats (e.g., paint), first treat with a sealer before painting. These include commercial sealers, lacquer, shellac, liquid plastic, etc. Let the sealer dry for 48 hours before painting.

Staining

When applying stain to plaster of Paris castings, wipe it off quickly with a soft flannel cloth. For darker shades, apply several coats, wiping each one off before applying the next coat.

Painting

Acrylic and oil paints are the most popular. Acrylic paint has one advantage over oil paint. It is a plastic base paint that eliminates the need for a sealer coat.

Spattering

There are two ways to create spattering. One way is for you to carefully knock a paint brush against a piece of window screen. The second is a commercial spray that produces a spattered pattern.

Flocking

Paint the surface of the plaster casting with flocking adhesive or liquid white glue, and cover with the flocking material. Carefully shake off any flocking not glued fast and let dry.

Antiquing

Although a little more complicated than some finishing techniques, antiquing is not difficult to do. You can buy inexpensive antiquing kits at most arts and crafts stores, paint dealers, and artist supply dealers.

Wire Brushing

Be careful when wire brushing plaster of Paris castings. Mistakes cannot be corrected. Decide in which direction the pattern is to flow, and carefully use a stiff wire brush. Practice on a scrap piece of plaster.

Modeling Clay

✔ You Will Need:

Potter's clay; glycerin; petroleum jelly; whiting.

◇ Preparation:

Potter's clay can be treated to make it pliable so that it will not dry out. Prepare a mixture of glycerin (2 parts by weight) and petroleum jelly (1 part by weight). Mix with the clay an knead to make a smooth mixture. Add more clay if too pliable. You can add whiting to lighten the color of the clay, but this will make your clay less pliable.

◆

Imitation Modeling Clay

✔ You Will Need:

Flowers of sulfur; lanolin; kaolin; glycerin.

◇ Preparation:

Mix 3 ounces of lanolin and 2 ounces of glycerin with 4 ounces of kaolin and 1 ounce of sulfur. Knead to make a smooth mixture. Add more sulfur if the texture is too thin. You can add dry paint color if you want. Use like any other clay except DO NOT ATTEMPT TO DRY USING HEAT.

◆

*

✔

◇

*

▭

Imitation Stone

✔ You Will Need:

Cement; sand; marble dust; water; dry earth colors.

◇ Preparation:

Mix cement (1 part by weight), sand (3 parts by weight) and marble dust (1 part by weight) with water to make a thick, pastelike mixture. To add color, dissolve it in the water before mixing with the dry ingredients. Pour your mixture into molds that you have coated with petroleum jelly. Let stand until set. Do not save any leftover stone; it will not keep. DO NOT FLUSH DOWN THE SINK. DISCARD IN A TRASH CAN.

◆

NEVER TASTE, DRINK, OR SMELL ANY OF THE CHEMICALS OR MIXTURES

Sand Casting

✔ You Will Need:

Sand; plaster of Paris; water.

◇ Preparation:

Dampen a mound of sand with water so it will pack easily and hold its shape. Scoop out the shape that will be cast. If you want to, you can line your mold with small pebbles, pieces of glass, stone tiles, shells, etc. Mix the plaster of Paris (see *How To Make Plaster Castings*). Fill the mold and let set. DO NOT TOUCH. THE PLASTER WILL BECOME HOT TO THE TOUCH. Let cool. Remove the casting and carefully brush off any loose sand. Rinse in water and dry using a soft cloth. Let harden for one week. Apply a sealer coat, and decorate with whatever colors you choose.

Plaster of Paris Dipping Mixture I

✔ You Will Need:

Plaster of Paris; powdered alum; water; petroleum jelly.

◇ Preparation:

Combine 3 cups of plaster of Paris and 2 teaspoons of alum with 2 cups of water (increase if necessary). Stir to form a smooth, creamy mixture.

HOW TO USE:

Dip cloth or paper strips into the plaster. Model over a bottle, dish, or other form that has been coated with petroleum jelly. Apply 3 to 4 layers. Work fast to shape the strips. The plaster will begin to set in 15 to 20 minutes. Let dry. When hard, separate from the form. Let dry for one week. Apply a sealer and paint if desired.

Plaster of Paris Dipping Mixture II

✔ You Will Need:

Plaster of Paris; powdered alum; spackling mixture; water; petroleum jelly.

◇ Preparation:

Combine 2 cups each of plaster of Paris, alum, and spackling mixture with 3 cups of water (increase if necessary). Stir to form a creamy mixture.

How To Use

See the preceding experiment, *Plaster of Paris Dipping Mixture I.* This mixture, however, takes longer to set, approximately 40 to 50 minutes. You will have time to correct any mistakes you make when positioning the materials. Let set and separate from the form. Let dry. Apply a sealer and paint if desired.

◆

Imitation Marble

✔ You Will Need:

Plaster of Paris; tempera paint; liquid white glue; water.

◇ Preparation:

Dissolve 1 tablespoon of glue in 1 cup of water. Stir in plaster of Paris to make a thick, lump free mixture that can be poured. Add tempera paint (the color depends on the color of the marble you want) onto the surface of the plaster. Fold (do not mix to blend) in the paint. Use this mixture as you would use other plaster mixtures for casting. Your castings made from this craft concoction are particularly strong and will have a smooth, marble texture.

◆

NEVER TASTE, DRINK, OR SMELL ANY OF THE CHEMICALS OR MIXTURES

Working with Plaster of Paris

Ornaments I

Inflate a balloon and tie tightly. Dip string or strips of cloth or paper in plaster (see *Plaster Of Paris Dipping Mixture I; Plaster Of Paris Dipping Mixture II*) and apply to the balloon. Let dry. Carefully pop the balloon to remove it. Let the casting dry for one week. Finish by gluing on decorations and/or painting. This is an excellent way for you to make mobiles and ornaments for holiday occasions.

Ornaments II

In a bottle with a narrow neck, mix plaster of Paris with water to make a smooth mixture that can be poured. Inflate a balloon and fasten it to the neck of the bottle. Invert and let the plaster of Paris pour into the balloon. Tie off the balloon and remove. Using gloves, remove the balloon and set aside to harden. When hard, carefully cut away the balloon and decorate.

Pipe Cleaner Sculptures

Twist pipe cleaners (or other wires) to make a three-dimensional skeleton of the object to be sculpted. Fasten to a base and carefully apply plaster of Paris or other modeling medium. When you work with colored mediums, let each color dry completely before you apply the next color. Do not remove the form.

Another Sculpture Method

Crumble newspaper or aluminum foil into shapes of objects that will be sculpted. Repeat the last experiment.

Carving Material I

✔ You Will Need:

Vermiculite; cement; sand; water; petroleum jelly.

◇ Preparation:

Mix vermiculite (8 parts by weight), cement (1 part by weight) and sand (1 part by weight) with water to make a thick paste. Pour into cardboard boxes coated with petroleum jelly. Let set. Remove and use as a carving material.

Carving Material II

✔ You Will Need:

Finely chopped soap; water; finely chopped crayons; waxed paper.

◇ Preparation:

Over low heat, melt 1 cup of soap in ¾ cup of water. Add 1 cup of crayon and stir until you get a uniform color. WEAR GLOVES. THE MIXTURE IS VERY HOT. Scrape the mixture into a box lined with waxed paper and let cool. Because this mixture is difficult to clean, use a pot that can be thrown away. When hard, remove the box and waxed paper. Use as a carving material.

Notes

✳

✔

◇

Papier Mache

✔ You Will Need:

Newspaper; wallpaper paste; nonrising flour; water.

◇ Preparation:

Cut newspaper into very small pieces. Soak in water for two or three days. Pour off the water and mix with equal amounts of paste and flour. Knead to form a smooth claylike mass. Objects made from this papier mache will air dry in approximately 1 week; longer for large ones. You should fill any cracks with the papier mache mixture. When it is dry, spray with clear, waterproof varnish and decorate with tempera paints.

◆

✳

▱

Papier Mache Strips

✔ You Will Need:

Newspaper; wallpaper strips; water.

◇ Preparation:

Cut newspaper into 1 inch wide strips. Pull a strip at a time through a thin mixture of wallpaper paste and water. Apply to an armature (see *Armatures*) or use with *Ornaments I, Pipe Cleaner Sculptures,* or *Another Sculpture Method.* Repeat with additional layers to get the thickness you want, usually at least 5 or 6 layers. Individual layers should be placed crosswise to each other. Let dry and spray with clear, waterproof varnish and decorate with tempera paints.

◆

Papier Mache Mash

✔ You Will Need:

Newspaper; plaster of Paris; liquid white glue; water.

◇ Preparation:

Tear 1 ounce of newspaper in small pieces and soak in water for 2 or 3 days. Pour off the water and add 3 tablespoons of glue, stirring until mixed. Add 3 to 4 ounces of plaster of Paris. Knead, adding water if necessary, until a smooth, lump free mass forms. Papier mache mash dries very fast to a hard, plastic looking finish and should be used as soon as possible after you prepare it. You can shape it with a modeling knife. Finish with paint, lacquer, or shellac. If you apply a sealer coat before painting, you will waterproof it.

Tips on Working With Papier Mache

• Papier mache articles will separate easier from molds coated with petroleum jelly.
• To make certain that each layer of papier mache covers the object, use alternating layers of different colored paper.
• Adding sand or sawdust to papier mache will produce unusual surface textures. If necessary, increase the paste.
• Large objects can be made stronger by using a layer of cloth strips (unbleached muslin) for one of paper.
• To make papier mache articles harder, paint with linseed oil and bake in an oven at 250 degrees until dry.
• Papier mache articles can be waterproofed by applying 2 or 3 coats of lacquer or waterproof shellac.
• Dried papier mache articles can be sandpapered smooth before finishing with shellac, paint, etc. Use fine, dry sandpaper.

Armatures

Often, when you are constructing objects using papier mache, you will need a foundation on which to build the modeling medium. In the craft world, they are called *armatures*. Armatures usually are 3-dimensional skeletons or rough shaped models upon which the papier mache is applied. Armatures can also be used with other craft modeling mediums. A few of the more popular types of armatures are:

1. Fold, twist, or tie newspaper into an approximate shape of the object you want. Apply the papier mache over the armature. When the papier mache is dry, it will strengthen the armature, making it rigid.

2. Cut cardboard or thin plywood and fasten together to make an armature. Then apply the papier mache and let it dry.

3. Use inflated balloons for perfect ovals, circles, etc. You can use one or a group. Apply the papier mache to them very carefully. After the form is dry, you can remove the balloons by popping them. Balloon armatures are an excellent way to make festive decorations.

4. You can use almost anything - bowls, boxes, bottles, or pieces of scrap wood. Always apply a coating of petroleum jelly, if the armature is to be removed, before modeling with papier mache.

5. If you want a large object such as a pinata, fasten together wire to make a skeleton. If the spaces between the wires are large, cover the form with screen wire. Apply the papier mache and let dry. Finish the object by painting and then gluing on decorations.

Paints

You can add color to create artistic beauty to your finished form. If you are interested in learning more about color and how it should be used, there are many excellent books on the subject that you can get from your local library. I have included a few of the more popular paints here. The formulas are easy to prepare and can be used with the projects listed in this book.

Finger Paint I

✔ You Will Need:

Cornstarch; gelatin; water; soap flakes; water soluble dye; borax.

◇ Preparation:

Soften 1 envelope of gelatin in ¼ cup of water. Sprinkle the gelatin on the surface of the water and let it stand for 15 minutes. Make a smooth paste of ½ cup of cornstarch in water. Add 2 cups of hot water to the starch and cook over low heat until the starch thickens. Remove from heat and stir in the gelatin. Add ¾ cup of soap flakes. Blend in the dye and add 1 teaspoon of borax as a preservative. If you store the paint in an airtight, glass container, it will keep for several weeks.

Finger Paint II

✔ You Will Need:

Cornstarch; water; borax; glycerin; food color.

◇ Preparation:

Prepare a smooth paste of 1 cup of cornstarch in ½ cup of water. Add 4 cups of hot water and stir over low heat until the starch thickens. Remove from the heat and add ½ teaspoon of borax dissolved in 1 cup of cold water. If it is too thick, add more water. Stir in 2 tablespoons of glycerin and enough food color to make the color of paint you want. If the paint is stored in airtight, glass containers, it will keep for several months.

Waterproof Poster Paint

✔ You Will Need:

Dry powdered nonfat milk; borax; dry paint color; water; powdered chalk.

◇ Preparation:

Sift 11 ounces of chalk, 6 teaspoons of milk and 1 teaspoon of borax. Mix with water to make a thick, creamlike mixture. Add dry paint color, stirring to blend. This paint will keep for several weeks when stored in a tightly capped glass jar. When the paint is dry, it is waterproof and permanent.

Powdered Milk Paint

✔ You Will Need:

Powdered nonfat milk; dry paint color; water.

◇ Preparation:

Combine 2 cups of milk and water. Let stand in a cool place to allow any foam that might form to disappear. Make a smooth mixture of a small amount of dry paint color and a little of the milk. Add this mixture to the rest of the milk. This paint will dry to a permanent, opaque finish. It will keep for 1 to 2 weeks when poured into a tightly capped glass jar and placed in the refrigerator.

Liquid Starch Poster Paint

✔ You Will Need:

Liquid laundry starch; food color.

◇ Preparation:

An easy to make poster paint can be prepared by mixing food color (or other water soluble dye) with liquid starch. Be sure you use it as soon as you've made it since this paint will spoil after a day or two.

Salt Paint

✔ You Will Need:

Salt; nonrising flour; food color; water.

◇ Preparation:

Combine 2 ounces of salt and 1 ounce of flour. Combine with water to make a thick suspension. To add color, dissolve food color (or other water soluble dye) in the water before mixing with the flour and salt. This makes an excellent slow drying paint for your relief pictures.

How To Use:

Use wood applicator sticks to apply the paint to an outlined drawing. Apply one color at a time and let it dry before beginning the next color. (See *Modeling Concoction; Modeling Paint*.)
SUGGESTION: If the paint is too thin, you can thicken it by adding flour.

Modeling Paint

✔ You Will Need:

Powdered tempera colors; dry wallpaper paste; liquid laundry starch.

◇ Preparation:

This is another excellent paint that you can use to make your relief pictures. Mix:

Powdered tempera color	2 cups
Wallpaper paste	4 tablespoons
Laundry starch	½ cup

If the mixture is too thin, add some more wallpaper paste.

How To Use:

See the preceding experiment, Salt Paint.

Coloring Materials

Food Colors

To Prepare		Mix (no. of drops)		
	GREEN	YELLOW	RED	BLUE
Orange		2	1	
Purple			3	1
Turquoise	1			3
Chartreuse	1	12		
Toast	1	4	3	
Violet			1	2

Household Laundry Dyes

Household laundry dyes (Rit, Tintex, etc.) are easy to use as coloring materials. Just follow the manufacturer's instructions for mixing, or try adding a few grains of the dry powder to water before adding it to the ingredients listed in other experiments.

Adhesives

If you enjoy working with paper projects, or want to start, you will find the recipes for adhesives interesting and very helpful when you combine them with other craft activities. You can do almost anything you can imagine with them.

Glue

✔ You Will Need:

Dextrin; borax; liquid glucose; water.

◇ Preparation: Wear Goggles

Dissolve 6 teaspoons of borax and 6 ounces of dextrin in 5 ounces of hot water. Add 5 teaspoons of glucose. Cook over low heat, stirring until it becomes a clear solution. If it is too thick, add hot water. Strain through gauze. You can keep this glue for several weeks if you store it in a tightly capped jar.

How To Use:

This is an excellent glue for fastening wood and paper to paper.

Casein Glue

✔ You Will Need:

Skim milk; vinegar; borax; water.

◇ Preparation:

Warm 8 cups of milk. While stirring, add just enough vinegar to separate the milk into curds (casein) and whey (liquid). Filter off the whey. Wash the casein three or four times with fresh water. Dissolve 4 teaspoons of borax in 6 tablespoons of water. Add the casein and let it stand until it dissolves and forms a smooth mixture. This will take a day or two. If the mixture is too thick, add a little hot water.

How To Use:

This is a waterproof glue that is permanent when dry. It is an excellent adhesive for general household use.

Waterproof Glue for Glass

✔ You Will Need:

Gelatin; skim milk; water; oil of wintergreen.

◇ Preparation:

Sprinkle 2 packets of gelatin over 2 tablespoons of warm water and set aside to soften. Heat 3 tablespoons of milk to boiling and stir to mix with the gelatin. Add a few drops of oil of wintergreen as a preservative.

How To Use:

This glue will jell when cool. To use, place it in a glass container and heat in a pan of water to soften. The adhesive properties of this glue makes it great for joining glass to glass, metal to glass, paper to glass, etc.

Paper Paste

✔ You Will Need:

Nonrising flour; powdered alum; sugar; water; sodium benzoate.

◇ Preparation:

Mix 1 cup of flour, 1 cup of sugar and 2 teaspoons of alum with water to make a smooth paste. Heat 18 ounces of water to boiling and slowly add the flour-sugar mixture. Cook over low heat, stirring until the mixture thickens. Add more water if it is too thick. Add 1 teaspoon of sodium benzoate as a preservative.

How To Use:

Stored in tightly covered glass jars, this paste will keep for several months without refrigeration. It is an excellent, all purpose adhesive for paper projects.

Household Paste

✔ You Will Need:

Nonrising flour; sugar; water; sodium benzoate.

◇ Preparation:

Combine 1 cup of flour and 6 tablespoons of sugar with 3 cups of water. Add the water in small amounts, stirring to make a smooth, lump free mixture. Cook over low heat, stirring constantly, until the mixture thickens and turns translucent. Add ½ teaspoon of sodium benzoate as a preservative.

How To Use:

This paste will keep on the shelf for several weeks if you store it in a tightly capped glass jar. It works well for all paper construction projects.

Wallpaper Paste

✔ You Will Need:

Nonrising flour; powdered alum, powdered rosin; water; oil of wintergreen.

◇ Preparation:

Mix 3 cups of flour; 3 tablespoons of alum and 3 tablespoons of rosin. Add 4 cups of warm water and stir to make a smooth paste. Add it to 14 cups of hot water and stir to prevent any lumps from forming. Cook over low heat until the mixture thickens. Thin with 4 to 5 cups of cold water. Add ¾ teaspoon of wintergreen oil as a preservative.

How To Use:

You can use this paste with papier mache, for pasting cloth to cardboard, and any other projects with paper that require a strong bond.

Mucilage I

✔ You Will Need:

Gum arabic; honey; water; oil of wintergreen.

◇ Preparation:

Mix 2 ounces of gum arabic with 8 ounces of hot water. Let stand 24 to 48 hours until dissolved. Strain off any lumps. Add 2 tablespoons of honey and 10 drops of oil of wintergreen.

How To Use:

This is not as strong as paste, but works well with paper projects.

Mucilage II

✔ You Will Need:

Gum arabic; cornstarch; sugar; water; oil of wintergreen.

◇ Preparation:

Mix 1 ounce of gum arabic with 4 ounces of hot water. Let stand for 24 to 48 hours until dissolved. Strain off any lumps. Add 1 tablespoon of sugar and 2 tablespoons of starch. Stir, and cook over low heat until the mixture thickens. If it is too thick, add hot water. Add 8 drops of oil of wintergreen as a preservative.

How To Use:

Mucilage II is stronger than Mucilage I and you can use it with many paper projects.

Chapter 7

Chemical Magic Grab Bag

This last chapter is an exciting collection of miscellaneous chemical and craft magic experiments - a grab bag. You can find all kinds of different, exotic experiments here; just keep reading and you will be amazed at what you will discover. Some of these experiments can be adapted to your chemical magic routines and others are more for your arts and crafts fun. Some even can help you make money.

Colored Flames

✻ The Effect:

Pine cones, wood chips, newspapers, and logs can be treated to make them burn with brilliant rainbow-hued colors.

✔ You Will Need:

Color producing chemicals-sodium chloride (yellow), strontium nitrate (red), lithium chloride (purple), calcium chloride (orange), potassium chloride (violet), borax (light green), copper sulfate (emerald green), barium nitrate (apple green), copper chloride (blue); newspapers; dried pine cones; sawdust; wood chips; aluminum foil; heavy string; water; logs.

◇ Preparation: Wear Goggles and Gloves

Prepare separate solutions by dissolving one pound of each chemical, separately, in one gallon of water.

◆

Mystery Logs I

Roll newspapers into tight, compact logs and tie them securely with string. Soak one log at a time in one of the solutions for several days until it is completely saturated. Keep covered to prevent evaporation. Remove and let dry. When you want to dazzle people with the brilliant colored flames, just place your mystery logs between regular logs in your fireplace and light them. The colored flames will burst into view. For a multicolored effect, try burning more than one log at a time.

◆

Mystery Logs II

Place sawdust in a cloth bag and soak for a few hours in one of the solutions. Weigh down the bag to keep it covered with water. Remove the bag and empty the sawdust onto newspaper to dry. Drill ½ inch holes, approximately 2 to 3 inches deep in the logs. Fill each hole with different treated sawdust and plug with aluminum foil. Add these treated logs to the regular logs and wait for the next time you have a fire. When you burn the logs, you will be treated to a rainbow display of colors.

Pine Cones

Place dried pine cones in a mesh bag and soak in one of the solutions for 48 hours. Weigh down the bag to keep it covered with water. Remove the cones and let them dry in a warm place. This may take several days. When you put them in the fireplace, you will get a vivid display of color. If you burn different cones at the same time, you will have several gorgeous colors at once.

Wood Chips

Repeat the last experiment, *Pine Cones,* using wood chips that are approximately 1 inch square and 5 to 6 inches long. For better results, you should use a soft, porous wood. Let the wood chips soak for at least 5 days. When they are dry, they will light up the fireplace with bursts of color.

Wear Goggles and Gloves

Art Masterpieces

✳ The Effect:

This experiment will give you the reputation of being a skilled artist who can create abstract art masterpieces.

✔ You Will Need:

Good grade art paper; toothpicks; oil base paint; water; shallow baking pan (approximately ¾ inch deep and slightly larger than the paper); paper towels; tweezers.

◇ Preparation:

Make sure that the pan is on a level surface and fill it with water to just below the edge. Dribble small amounts of paint onto the surface of the water. Do not use more than 2 or 3 colors. Carefully pass a toothpick through the paints to mix them. DO NOT OVERMIX. Lay a sheet of paper on the paint. Press gently to ensure full contact between the paper and paint. Hold in place for several seconds. Carefully remove the paper by pulling it by a corner with the tweezers. Let your masterpiece dry on paper towels, paint side up.

Making A Hectograph

✳ The Effect:

How to use a few everyday materials to make a simple and effective device for copying.

✔ You Will Need:

Gelatin; glycerin; sodium bicarbonate; water; shallow baking pan (approximately ½ inch deep and slightly larger than the paper).

◇ Preparation:

Dissolve ¼ ounce of sodium bicarbonate in 6-½ ounces of water. Add 3 ounces of gelatin, letting it stand for 2 or 3 hours to soften. Cook in a double boiler, without stirring, to dissolve the gelatin. When it has dissolved, stir to thoroughly disperse the gelatin in the water and add 18 ounces of glycerin. Cook until the solution clears. Do not let the temperature go over 145 degrees. Let cool to approximately 120 degrees. Pour into a pan and let stand until the mixture sets.

Using A Hectograph

✳ The Effect:

See the preceding experiment, *Making a Hectograph.*

✔ You Will Need:

Hectograph; hectograph ink or stencil paper; water; paper; soft sponge.

How To Use:

Follow the manufacturer's instructions for making an original document using hectograph ink or paper. Dampen the surface of the hectograph with a soft sponge and cool water. Place the original, ink side down, onto the hectograph. Leave in place for 1 or 3 seconds, then remove. Usually you can make several copies from one inking. When finished, gently wash the gelatin surface with a soft sponge and cool water. Let dry before using it again. Store it in a refrigerator, but be sure it doesn't freeze.

Magic With Crystals

Frosting Glass

✳ The Effect:

You can decorate glass with lacy, Jack Frost patterns.

✔ You Will Need:

Magnesium sulfate; dextrin; water; window glass; clear lacquer.

◇ Preparation:

Dissolve 6 tablespoons of magnesium sulfate in a solution of 2 tablespoons of dextrin in 8 ounces of water. Paint clean glass with the dextrin. Let the solution evaporate and a pattern of magnesium sulfate crystals will form. Spray with lacquer to preserve the pattern.

Crystal Patterns

✳ The Effect:

How to make patterns of colorful crystals.

✔ You Will Need:

Magnesium sulfate; dextrin; water; food colors; lacquer; heavy cardboard.

◇ Preparation:

Outline a picture on heavy cardboard. Repeat the experiment, *Frosting Glass,* adding a few drops of food coloring to the magnesium sulfate solution. Prepare as many different colored solutions as you need. Working with one solution at a time, paint all the sections of one color at one time. Let the first color dry before you start the next. When your colorful picture is finished, you can spray it with lacquer to preserve it.

Creeping Crystals

✳ The Effect:

How to make colorful crystal growths.

✔ You Will Need:

Magnesium sulfate; food colors; water.

◇ Preparation: Wear Goggles

Stir 4 ounces of magnesium sulfate in 4 ounces of water while heating at a low temperature. While it is still warm, carefully fill small containers (custard dishes, jar lids, soda bottle caps, etc.) up to the edge. In a few days, as the solution evaporates, colorful crystal growths will appear, bubbling over the edge of the container. If you store them in a dry place, they should last for several months.

The Magic Garden

✳ The Effect:

This project is a classic among chemical magic experiments. You can make stonelike materials grow into exotic, jungle-looking growths of mysterious colors.

✔ You Will Need:

Sodium chloride; laundry bluing; soapless household ammonia; mercurochrome; water; coke or charcoal briquets; food colors.

◇ Preparation:

Prepare the following mixture:

Sodium chloride	6 tablespoons
Laundry bluing	6 tablespoons
Ammonia	1 tablespoon
Water	6 tablespoons

Arrange 3 or 4 briquets in a shallow dish. Pour the mixture over the briquets. Add a few drops of mercurochrome to each briquet and let stand in the shade for several hours. Colorful crystal growths will appear. If you want to save these crystals, all you have to do is add a sodium chloride solution (1 tablespoon in a little water) to the crystals each day.
SUGGESTION: For a multicolored effect, replace the mercurochrome with food colors, using several colors in the same dish.

Magic Forests

✳ The Effect:

Colorful stones grow into beautiful underwater gardens.

✔ You Will Need:

Sodium silicate solution; large crystals or lumps of ferric chloride, cobalt chloride, copper nitrate, potassium ferrocyanide and calcium chloride; distilled water.

◇ Preparation: Wear Goggles and Gloves

Dilute 16 ounces of sodium silicate solution with 16 ounces of water. Fill a deep jar, fish bowl or other similar glass container with the solution. Carefully drop a few crystals of the above chemicals into the solution. In a few minutes, an almost miraculous transformation takes place. The crystals grow into a rain forest of different colors. When they stop growing, carefully siphon off the water and refill with fresh water. If you leave this forest undisturbed and not exposed to bright light or heat, it will bloom for a long time.

A Silver Tree

✳ The Effect:

You can almost grow a silver tree underwater through the miracle of chemistry.

✔ You Will Need:

Silver nitrate; tin strips; distilled water.

◇ Preparation: Wear Goggles and Gloves

Dissolve 4 teaspoons of silver nitrate in 1 ounce of water. Fill a glass cylinder with the solution and suspend in it a strip of tin (approximately ½ inch wide, and long enough to reach 1 inch from the bottom). The tin must be clean and polished. You can do this with steel wool and water. Shortly after you dangle the tin in the water, a tree with branches of bright silver crystals will appear in your bowl.

129

A Tree of Lead

✳ The Effect:

This experiment is similar to the *Tree of Silver,* but with this one you get the effect of a tree of lead.

✔ You Will Need:

Lead acetate; dilute acetic acid; zinc strips; distilled water.

◇ Preparation:

Dissolve 2 tablespoons of lead acetate in 16 ounces of water. If cloudy, add a few drops of dilute acetic acid. Fill a glass jar with the lead acetate and suspend in it a strip of zinc (approximately ½ inch wide, and long enough to reach 1 inch from the bottom). You can clean the zinc with steel wool and water. In a few hours, a delicate, featherlike growth of lead crystals will form, attaching themselves to the zinc, where they will continue to grow for several days.

Soap Bubble Solution

✳ The Effect:

How to make a solution that will give you stronger, longer lasting soap bubbles.

✔ You Will Need:

Liquid detergent (do not use soap); corn syrup; glycerin; water.

◇ Preparation:

Prepare the following solution:

Detergent	2 ounces
Corn syrup	¼ teaspoon
Glycerin	4 tablespoons
Water	4 ounces

How To Use:

Bend a coat hanger wire into a ¾ inch loop with a 6 inch handle. Dip the loop into the solution, remove it, gently wave it through the air, and watch the stream of delicate bubbles float out.

◆

NEVER TASTE, DRINK, OR SMELL ANY OF THE CHEMICALS OR MIXTURES

Notes

* ━━━━━━━━━━
  ━━━━━━━━━━
  ━━━━━━━━━━
  ━━━━━━━━━━
✔ ━━━━━━━━━━
  ━━━━━━━━━━
  ━━━━━━━━━━
  ━━━━━━━━━━
◇ ━━━━━━━━━━
  ━━━━━━━━━━
  ━━━━━━━━━━
  ━━━━━━━━━━
* ━━━━━━━━━━
  ━━━━━━━━━━
  ━━━━━━━━━━
  ━━━━━━━━━━
▭ ━━━━━━━━━━
  ━━━━━━━━━━
  ━━━━━━━━━━
  ━━━━━━━━━━

Picture Copying Solution

✳ The Effect:

This is an excellent, fun producing activity particularly for those rainy days when you are stuck indoors. With this solution, you can easily make copies of pictures.

✔ You Will Need:

Yellow laundry soap; turpentine; water.

◇ Preparation:

Dissolve 2 teaspoons of soap in 20 ounces of hot water. Add 5 teaspoons of turpentine and shake to mix.

How To Use:

This solution can be used to copy pictures from newspapers and pulp magazines. Using a soft brush or cotton, apply the solution evenly over the picture to be copied. Blot away any excess, then place the picture, treated side down, onto a sheet of paper. Make sure the paper is resting on a hard surface. Rub firmly and evenly over the back of the picture using the bowl of a spoon. Remove the picture to reveal a mirror image copy.

Leaf Prints

✳ The Effect:

This next project can start you off on a whole new hobby collecting prints of different types of leaves.

✔ You Will Need:

Carbon paper; newspaper; white bond paper; leaves; an iron.

◇ Preparation:

Cover your work area with newspaper. Place a leaf, vein side down, onto a sheet of carbon paper. Cover the leaf with a second sheet of newspaper. Gently press the paper with an iron set at its lowest temperature. Replace the carbon paper with a sheet of white paper and again press with the iron. When you remove the leaf, you will reveal a print that will last long after the leaf itself has withered away.

* ✱
* ✔
* ◇
* ✱
* ▭

Sand Painting

✱ The Effect:

How to make colored sand pictures.

✔ You Will Need:

Washed white sand; water soluble dyes (see *Coloring Materials*); liquid white glue; mounting surfaces (heavy paper or cardboard, masonite, plywood, metal, etc.); newspaper.

◇ Preparation:

Color sand by soaking it in different dye solutions. Remove and spread on newspaper to dry. To sand paint a picture:

1. Lightly outline a picture on the mounting material.

2. Apply glue to the areas with the same color.

3. Carefully sprinkle sand onto the glue. Let dry.

4. Repeat with the next color.

5. Fill in all the areas to produce a picture.

◆

Melted Crayon Prints

✱ The Effect:

How to make art prints using ordinary crayons.

✔ You Will Need:

Wax crayons; aluminum foil; food warming tray; good grade of art paper; oven mittens.

◇ Preparation:

Cover a food warming tray set at medium heat with aluminum foil. Using crayons, draw a picture on the foil. The crayons will melt as the picture is drawn. Cover with a sheet of paper and carefully smooth out any wrinkles. Wearing gloves, gently press down on the paper and hold in place for 2 or 3 seconds. Lift off and a copy of the picture will appear on the paper.

◆

Crayon Melts

✳ The Effect:

Another version of the preceding experiment.

✔ You Will Need:

Wax crayons; wax paper; an iron; cloth; heavy wood board.

◇ Preparation:

Place a sheet of wax paper on a wood board covered with cloth. Arrange on the paper tiny pieces of crayon and colored string, thread, tissue paper, leaves etc. Cover with a second sheet of wax paper and cloth. Press with an iron set on low heat until the crayons melt. Let cool and remove the cloth to reveal a picture.

◆

Weather Barometer

✳ The Effect:

Combining a few chemicals, a mixture can be prepared that can be used to predict possible weather conditions.

✔ You Will Need:

Cobalt chloride; sodium chloride; calcium chloride; gum arabic; water; blotting paper.

◇ Preparation:

Prepare the following solution:

Cobalt chloride	5 teaspoons
Sodium chloride	3 teaspoons
Calcium chloride	1 teaspoon
Water	2 ounces

Mix 1 teaspoon of gum arabic with 2 ounces of hot water and let stand for 24 to 48 hours until it dissolves. Strain off any lumps. Add 1 ounce of the gum arabic solution to the cobalt chloride solution. Saturate blotting paper and air dry at room temperature.

How To Use:

Expose the paper to air. Depending on how much moisture is in the air, color changes will occur that you can use to predict the weather as follows:

Blue	Dry
Lavender blue	Dry to damp
Blue red	Damp
Pink	Wet
Rose red	Rain

◗ What Happens:

Calcium chloride and sodium chloride absorb moisture from the air. With moisture, cobalt chloride turns pink to rose red. It changes to the other colors as the moisture decreases.

Spirit Writing Pad

✳ The Effect:

You can make a magic pad on which writing disappears, leaving the pad clean to be used again.

✔ You Will Need:

White paraffin; heavy black poster board; celluloid; stapler; blunt wood pencil shaped stick.

◇ Preparation:

Using a double boiler, melt the wax over low heat. BE CAREFUL. MELTED WAX IS HOT. Coat one side of the poster board with the wax. Let harden. Loop a 1 inch wide strip of poster board around the wax treated board. Staple it closed. It should be loose enough so it can slide up and down. Staple a sheet of celluloid to the top edge of the board, over the cardboard loop.

How To Use:

Write on the celluloid using the blunt wood pencil shaped stick. Writing will appear. To make the writing vanish, slide the cardboard loop up and down over the writing, separating the celluloid cover from the board. The pad can be used to write another message.

✳

✔

◇

✳

▭

Notes

Sand Candles

☀ The Effect:

How to cast candles in sand molds.

✔ You Will Need:

Paraffin wax; wax crayons; large pot; kitchen candles; oven mittens; source of heat; empty cans at least 4 to 5 inches wide; water; sand; stearic acid; wood stirrers.

◇ Preparation:

This is a great fun project for you to do at the beach. Fill a box with sand. Scoop out the shape of the candle to be poured. Melt wax in a can placed in boiling water. BE CAREFUL. MELTED WAX IS HOT. USE MITTENS TO HOLD THE CAN. Add small pieces of crayon to color the wax and stir to mix. Lift out the can and pour the wax into the mold. To insert a wick, before pouring the wax, stand a candle upright in the indentation. Let cool and remove the candle from the sand. Brush off any loose sand. SUGGESTION: For candles that will burn slower with less dripping, add 2 ounces of stearic acid to each 3 pounds of wax.

Egg In The Bottle

☀ The Effect:

You show your audience a bottle containing an egg larger than the bottle's opening. Everyone wonders how you accomplished this magic.

✔ You Will Need:

Raw egg with shell intact; dilute acetic acid; empty milk bottle.

◇ Preparation:

Dissolve away the shell of the egg by treating it with acetic acid for several days. It might be necessary to change the acid several times. This will leave the egg protected only by a heavy membrane. Carefully, pushing very gently, force the egg into the bottle. In a few days the egg will harden as the membrane absorbs carbon dioxide from the air. And the illusion is now complete.

◆

The Knotty Bone

✳ The Effect:

You can treat chicken bones so that they can be tied in knots.

✔ You Will Need:

Chicken bones washed clean; dilute acetic acid.

◇ Preparation:

Repeat the last experiment, *Egg in the Bottle,* using chicken bones in place of the egg. When the bones are soft, remove them from the acid and wash clean. Tie them in knots and set aside to let them harden.

◆

✳

✔

◇

✳

▭

Elixir of Life

✳ The Effect:

What looks like sand is dropped into water. Suddenly the sand appears to become alive, moving about like living bugs. Touch the water with a finger and they stop as if all magical life has vanished.

✔ You Will Need:

Camphor; distilled water.

◇ Preparation:

Crumble the camphor into small, grain-like pieces.

✳ Presentation:

Drop a few pieces of the camphor into a dish of water and watch them move and dart about like live insects. Touch the surface of the water with the end of your finger, and they suddenly stop as if all life has vanished.

⬭ What Happens:

Camphor reacts with water to release hydrogen, causing the particles to move around. Touching the water with your finger, which has oil on it, coats the water with a film of oil. This prevents the camphor from coming in contact with water, stopping the reaction.

◆

Dry Water

✳ The Effect:

Placing your hands in a bowl of water, you remove an object with your hands still completely dry.

✔ You Will Need:

Lycopodium powder.

◇ Preparation:

Have someone drop a coin into a bowl of water.

✳ Presentation:

Drop about 1 teaspoonful of lycopodium powder into the water. Wait a few seconds, then reach into the water and remove the coin. The coin is wet, YOUR HAND IS DRY!

▭ What Happens:

The lycopodium powder spreads to cover the surface of the water. It acts as a waterproof glove, keeping the water away from the hand when it is placed in it. Since the coin is already in the water before the lycopodium has been added, it is wet and remains wet when removed from the bowl.

◆

Blushing Photograph

✳ The Effect:

Showing a photograph or drawing of a lady, suddenly her face turns red, as if she were blushing.

✔ You Will Need:

Phenolphthalein solution; amonium hydroxide; photograph or drawing.

◇ Preparation:

Paint the face of the lady in the photograph with the phenolphthalein, and let dry.

✳ Presentation:

When ready to perform the experiment, expose the picture for a few seconds to the vapors from the ammonium hydroxide. A red color (blushing) appears.

◗ What Happens:

Phenolphthalein, an indicator, turns red with a base (ammonium hydroxide).

◆

Mysterious Sugar Cubes

✳ The Effect:

Lump sugar usually dissolves when placed into coffee or tea, or other liquids. This sugar floats without dissolving, no matter how much the liquid is stirred.

✔ You Will Need:

Flexible Collodion.

◇ Preparation:

Coat several lumps of sugar by dipping them into flexible collodion. Hold the sugar with pointed tweezers. Set aside to dry, and repeat two or three more times. It will be almost impossible to see the preparation.

✳ Presentation:

Secretly substitute the prepared sugar for those that are unprepared. Unsuspecting persons will be bewildered when they observe that sugar will not dissolve as described in The Effect.

⌐ What Happens:

Flexible collodion forms a waterproof coating on the sugar, preventing it from dissolving or sinking.

———————————— ◆ ————————————

Floating Soap Bubbles

✳ The Effect:

How to levitate soap bubbles in mid air without any visible means of support.

✔ You Will Need:

Dry ice; soap bubble solution; bubble pipe; deep dish.

◇ Preparation:

Place a small piece of dry ice in a dish and let it evaporate. USE PAPER TO HANDLE DRY ICE.

✳ Presentation:

Blow soap bubbles into the dish. Instead of falling to the bottom, they mysteriously float in mid air, as if on an invisible surface.

⌐ What Happens:

Dry ice is solid carbon dioxide. In its gaseous state it is invisible. Heavier than air, it remains in the dish. The soap bubbles, being lighter than the carbon dioxide, appear to float in mid air, but are actually floating on the surface of the invisible carbon dioxide.

———————————— ◆ ————————————

Perpetual Magic Motion

✳ The Effect:

You can use magic to accomplish many things, including perpetual motion.

✔ You Will Need:

Carbonated soda water; glass; washed apple seeds.

✱ Presentation:

Fill a tall glass with soda water. Drop in several apple seeds. They will sink to the bottom, only to rise to the top, and then sink again. This continues for several minutes.

◗ What Happens:

Soda water contains dissolved carbon dioxide that appears as bubbles. These attach to the seeds, making them buoyant. When this happens, the seeds float to the top. At the top the carbon dioxide escapes, the seeds lose their buoyancy and sink to the bottom. The rising and sinking continues as long as there is carbon dioxide present.

Strange Water

✳ The Effect:

White stones dropped into a glass of water change to an almost black color.

✔ You Will Need:

Laundry starch lumps; tincture of iodine; water.

◇ Preparation:

Fill a tall glass with 1 pint of water and secretly add 18 drops of iodine.

✳ Presentation:

Bring out the glass of water with the iodine, along with several lumps of starch and drop them into the glass. As they sink to the bottom, they change from a white color to one that is almost black.

▭ What Happens:

Iodine is used to test for starch. The appearance of a blue-black to black color is a positive test for iodine.
SUGGESTION: In the event the color change is too slow, increase the iodine; if it is too fast, decrease it.

✳

✔

◇

✳

◗

Sun Pictures

✳ The Effect:

First used over 200 years ago to make one of the first pictures, you can do the same thing with twentieth century materials.

✔ You Will Need:

Kodak Studio Proof "F" Paper (or another similar product); opaque objects (keys, lace, leaves, paper tracings, etc.); sodium thiosulfate; distilled water; window glass.

◇ Preparation:

Under subdued light (red if possible), arrange opaque objects on a sheet of proof paper. THIS PAPER IS LIGHT SENSITIVE AND MUST NOT BE EXPOSED TO LIGHT UNTIL READY TO USE. Cover flat objects (lace, or tracings) with glass. Make certain that any other paper not being used is covered. Expose to bright light (bulb or sunlight) until the uncovered sections turn brownish-purple. Remove the objects and a picture of them will remain. To make the pictures permanent, treat the paper for 5 to 10 minutes in a solution of sodium thiosulfate (4 teaspoons dissolved in 6 ounces of water). Wash in a slow stream of cool water for 15 to 20 minutes. Press dry between blotters or paper towels.

◗ What Happens:

When early scientists first made these pictures, they used paper coated with light sensitive silver compounds. Kodak Studio Proof "F" Paper is a modern replacement for yesterday's light sensitive paper. Light changes the silver compounds to non-light sensitive metallic silver. Sodium thiosulfate fixes (makes permanent) the photograph by converting the unexposed silver compounds to water soluble silver salts. These are removed by washing with water.

Blueprints

✳ The Effect:

How to make pictures using another light sensitive process.

✔ You Will Need:

Blueprint paper; clear window glass; opaque objects (keys, lace, leaves, paper tracings, etc.); water.

◇ Preparation:

Arrange the opaque objects on a sheet of blueprint paper under subdued light. THIS PAPER IS LIGHT SENSITIVE AND MUST NOT BE EXPOSED TO BRIGHT LIGHT UNTIL YOU ARE READY TO USE IT. Cover flat objects with glass. Expose the paper to bright light for several minutes. Because the strength of the light can vary, you might have to conduct some tests to determine the correct exposure time. To develop the picture, wash the paper in cool running water until a white picture appears. Blot dry. No further treatment is necessary; the picture will not fade.

◖ What Happens:

Blueprint paper contains light sensitive ferric ammonium citrate that changes, upon exposure to light, to non-light sensitive ferrous ammonium citrate. This reacts with potassium ferrocyanide to form insoluble, non-light sensitive Turnbull's blue. Washing the print removes any unreacted light sensitive chemical compounds, resulting in a white picture with a blue background.

Blueprint Paper

✳ The Effect:

How to make blueprint paper. YOU WILL NEED:
Potassium ferrocyanide; green ferric ammonium citrate;
water; bond paper.

◇ Preparation:

Under subdued light prepare the following solutions:

| No. 1 | 2 tablespoons potassium ferrocyanide in 4 ounces water |
| No. 2 | 2 tablespoons ferric ammonium citrate in 4 ounces water |

Mix the two solutions and pour into a glass dish. Holding 6
inch squares of paper by the corner, draw them one at a
time, over the surface of the solution. Make certain that
only one side is coated. Let dry, sensitive side up, on paper
towels and store in a lightproof box.

How To Use:

See *Blueprints*.

◆

Photographic Drawings

✳ The Effect:

You can change photographic prints into pen and ink
sketches.

✔ You Will Need:

Potassium iodide; iodine crystals; sodium thiosulfate;
distilled water; waterproof drawing ink; slightly

underexposed photographic print on smooth, matte paper; pen.

◇ Preparation:

Prepare the following solutions:

| No. 1 | ¼ oz. iodine, ¼ oz. potassium iodide, 5 oz. water. |
| No. 2 | 1 oz. sodium thiosulfate, 20 oz. water. |

Outline the highlights of a photograph with drawing ink. Let dry. Under subdued light place the photograph in solution No. 1 and gently rock it until the photograph fades. Remove and rinse a few seconds in water. Place the print in the sodium thiosulfate, leaving it until it turns white. Remove and wash in cool running water for 10 to 15 minutes. Press dry between blotters. A pen and ink sketch will replace the original photograph.

⟁ What Happens:

Iodine and potassium iodide react with the metallic silver in the photograph to form silver iodide. This reacts with the sodium thiosulfate to form a complex, water soluble compound that is removed when washed with water, leaving your pen and ink sketch.

◆

Printing Photos on Cloth

✳ The Effect:

How to print your photos onto cloth. Great for making unique scarves!

✔ You Will Need:

Ferric ammonium citrate; tartaric acid; silver nitrate; distilled water; sodium thiosulfate; silk cloth; brush; clear window glass; rubber bands; photographic negative.

◇ Preparation: Wear Gloves

Dissolve the following, each in separate 6 ounce portions of water:

Ferric ammonium citrate	90	grams
Tartaric acid	15	grams
Silver nitrate	37.5	grams

Under subdued light, mix the ferric ammonium sulfate and tartaric acid. Slowly add the silver nitrate with stirring. Dilute with water to make 1000 ml. This light sensitive solution will keep for about 3 months if stored in a tightly capped amber bottle and put in a cool place.

How To Use:

To sensitize silk cloth, coat one side of the fabric by brushing on the solution with cotton or a soft brush. Keep in a dark place. To print a picture, place a photographic negative (emulsion side down) on the cloth. Place between two sheets of glass and fasten with rubber bands. Expose to bright light. Stop when details of the picture become visible in the highlight areas. Wash in cool running water for no longer than 2 minutes. Fix for 2 or 3 minutes in a solution of sodium thiosulfate (1 ounce dissolved in 20 ounces of water). Do not over fix or the picture will fade. Wash in cool running water for 15 minutes and let dry.

▭ What Happens:

A complex, light sensitive iron and silver compound forms that changes to a non-light sensitive compound when exposed to light. Sodium thiosulfate combines with the unchanged light sensitive salts to form a water soluble compound that is removed when the cloth is washed in water.

Glossary

Absorb the process of taking in a substance and holding it fast.

Acid a compound that contains hydrogen and will combine chemically with common metals to form other compounds.

Base a compound that can burn the skin and will combine with an acid to form a salt (compound) and water.

cc. cubic centimeters, a unit of measurement with respect to liquids.

Chemiluminescence the production of light at low temperatures.

Complex Compound A compound that contains two or more different substances that are in combination with each other.

Dehydration the process of removing water from a substance.

Dilute to weaken or reduce the strength of a substance.

Distilled water water that has been purified by evaporation and condensation in order to remove minerals and other impurities.

Evaporate the process by which a liquid changes to a gas.

Extract to separate or otherwise obtain a specific substance from a mixture.

Filter the process of passing a liquid through a porous material (having many tiny openings) to separate out suspended impurities, or to recover solid matter.

Fluorescence the production of visible light upon exposure of a substance to light.

Indicator a substance used to indicate the presence of an acid or base.

Inflammable a substance capable of being set on fire and made to burn.

Jell   the jellylike state of a substance that has solidified.

Legerdemain   the act of performing magic through the use of sleight of hand or other trickery.

Light sensitive   the property of a substance that enables it to undergo change upon exposure to light.

Matte paper   paper that has a dull finish.

Neutralize   the process of making a solution neutral by the addition of an acid to a base, or a base to an acid.

Opaque   the condition of a substance that will not allow light to pass through it.

Perpetual motion   Motion produced by a machine that does not use up energy or create friction.

Potpourri   an sweet smelling mixture of dried petals (usually roses) mixed with spices and herbs.

Precipitate   a solid substance produced by the mixing of two or more solutions.

Reaction   the result when two or more chemicals are mixed.

Saturated   the state of a solution when it contains the maximum amount of a substance that will dissolve in it at a specific temperature.

Spectrum   an arrangement of the different colors that make up white light.

Suspension   a finely divided insoluble solid in a liquid that is very slow to settle out.

Tbsp.   tablespoon.

Texturizing   the addition of different materials to craft mediums to make unusual surface textures.

Translucent   the passage of light through materials, with such light becoming diffused, preventing the identification of objects behind it.

Tsp.   teaspoon.

Unglazed paper   Paper that has not been coated with a film or other material.

About The Author:

Edward Palder is the author of several other books on Chemistry for kids including the best-selling *Magic With Chemistry* published by Grosset & Dunlop. He is also the author of *The Catalog of Catalogs*. A man of diverse interests, Mr. Palder has been a professional magician, scientist, pharmacist, and, of course, author.